I created this study guide, because I realized that when adults who have been unchurched come to Christ, many times the church assumes this new believer has been granted all doctrinal understanding through the Holy Spirit. This is an attempt to get those new believers up to speed, so they have an understanding of what we, as Christians, believe and why. This is only a bird's eye view of the entire Bible. My prayer is this book will inspire the reader to seek God, through His word on their own.

Nick Martin

Lesson 1 – Introduction to the Bible

1. **The living word of God** – The Bible is not just a 2000 year old book, it is the living word of God (John1:1) As we mature in our walk with Jesus, we will discern new insights from scripture. The Bible is like a cell phone that links us directly to God. A one and done attitude of reading the Bible does not work, it is living and interacts with us, the more we interact with it.

2. **GAP - Time, Culture, Language** – Since the Bible is so old, there are some gaps we have to close in order to fully appreciate and understand what is written. These gaps are as follows:
    a. **Time** – There is approximately 6000 years from the time of Genesis until today. Times have changed drastically in the past 50 years, imagine how things (technology, science, world knowledge, and the super natural) have changed over 6000 years. We have to remind ourselves that these things looked a lot different to the people of the Old Testament than they do now.
    b. **Culture** – Cultures not only change over time, but over location as well. The Bible was not written under our Western ideology, it was written in the Middle East, under an Eastern ideology. We may think cultural standards, such as the role of women, may seem barbaric by today's standards, but they were accepted as the norm in that time and part of the world. We need to be careful not to impose our ideology onto scripture, that would have been completely unheard of during the times of the authors.
    c. **Language** – Of course we know the Bible wasn't written in English. Hebrew, Greek and Aramaic were the languages of the original texts. Unfortunately, words or ideas have a difficult time being translated into another language. Example – The Hebrew alphabet is also a numerical system as well as musical notes. The English language has three tenses for our verbs (past, present, and future). The Greek text has seven tenses for their verbs. Sometimes, there's just no English word for a Hebrew or Greek word, or phrase.

3. **Authors of the Bible, why so many?** There are 66 books that span 4000 years. God has revealed Himself to His people throughout the ages, and continues to do so today.

4. **Can the Bible be completely true?** Even though there were many people who put pen to paper, so to speak, the entire Bible was inspired by God. He gave the authors the words to write and they were faithful to convey His Message.

5. **Importance of genre - Exodus 3:3, Isaiah 55:12** The image on the following page shows the different genres that each book is written. It's important to know what genre we're reading, to understand the intent of the author. It would be like reading a Superman comic with the same intent and understanding as reading the Encyclopedia Britannica. The scripture examples above illustrate this. In Exodus, God spoke to Moses through a burning bush. This is factual and historical. The hills singing, and trees clapping their hands in Isaiah are metaphorical and are meant to represent the worship that all creation gives to God. It didn't really happen

6. **Importance of the Old Testament. Do we still need the Old Testament?** The Old Testament is the very foundation of our faith. Without it, our faith would fall flat. We'll discuss the importance of the Old Testament context to the New Testament later, when we get into the New Testament part of the study.

7. **Importance of Dead Sea Scrolls (1946-47 discovery)** The was criticism about the validity of the Old Testament up until the discovery of these scrolls. The issue critics proposed was that there was no evidence the Old Testament was actually written before the New Testament. They believed

the Old Testament was fabricated to make Jesus look like he was the supernatural Messiah. There was no way 351 prophecies about Jesus could have actually been fulfilled. History confirms the inhabitants of Qumran, where the scrolls were discovered, lived there and were disbanded 200 years before Jesus. These scrolls contained the entirety of the Old Testament we know today, with the exception of the book of Ester.

8. **Role of the New Testament.** The New Testament is a record of God's redemptive plan put into action. We will get more in depth as we go through those 13 lessons.

9. **Everything points to Jesus.** The entire Bible points to Jesus and His redemptive work in the past, present and future.

10. **Personal relationship through the Bible - Differing denominations** As we discussed earlier, due to many factors, translating the Bible to English can leave some understanding up to debate. As we go through this study, we will try to be as open as possible about the varying understandings in those difficult passages.

11. **Why so many translations of the Bible? – Formal, Functional, Paraphrase** The chart a couple of pages away shows most of the common English translations that are in use today. Formal (Word for Word) tries to translate as closely as possible to a word for word translation. This sometimes makes it difficult for us to understand, however. The Functional area (thought for thought) tries to stay as close to the original translation as possible, but in those difficult areas where words and phrases don't translate well, they use the author's intent over the actual words written. The paraphrase section throws translation out th window and writes from the authors intent, rather than the actual word. The small numbers by each translation at the bottom of the chart is the reading grade recommendation for that translation. Any serious Bible study will review scripture from two different forms of translation to get a better overall view of what the passage is talking about.

12. **Which version of the Bible is the best?** The best translation is the one you will read and can understand. They're all the word of God.

13. **Tools to help study. Devotionals, Commentaries, and Concordance -** There are many tools to help in our study of the Bible. Devotionals are a great way to stay in the word daily. They typically give a short passage and offer special insight. Commentaries are longer, sometimes huge books and go more in depth on a particular book or subject. A concordance is like a dictionary. It lists the English word, along with the original Hebrew or Greek and the original meaning of that word.

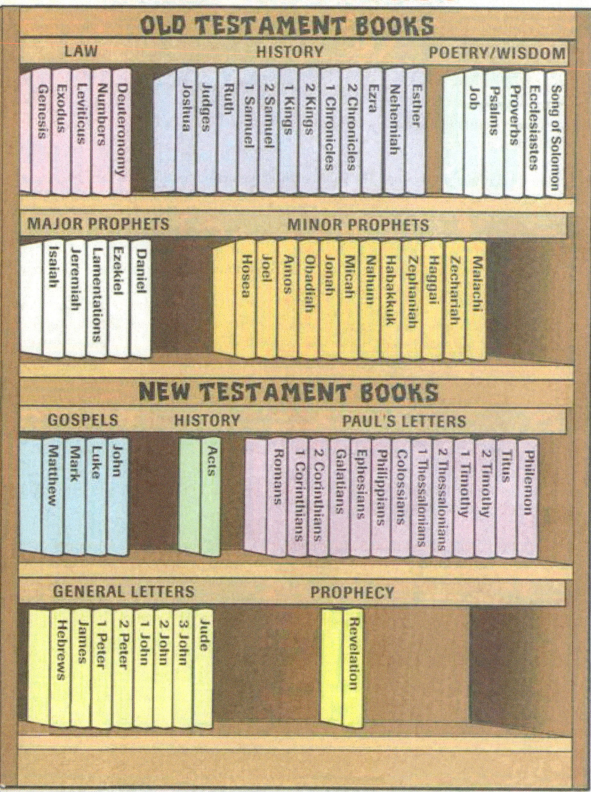

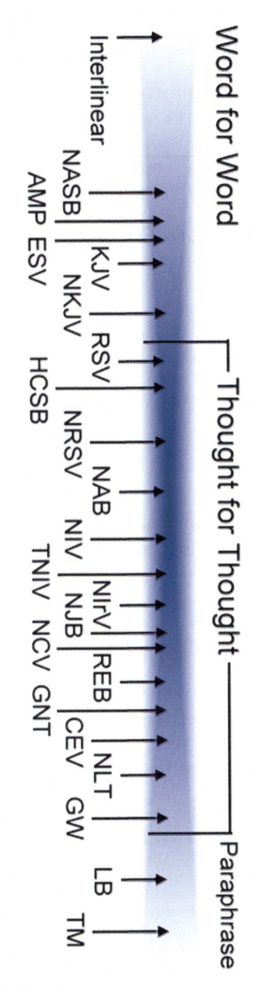

Lesson 2 – The Beginning
Genesis Chapters 1 & 2

- What does the introduction of light tell you about God? What clues about Him are found in the way He created the universe?

- What are the differences between Chapter 1 and Chapter 2? Why do you think Moses wrote two different versions of the same event?

- How did the creation of man differ from the rest of creation? What did God say about creating man? What do you think "Let us make man in our image" meant?

- What was the only thing God claimed was <u>not</u> good? What was Eve's role?

- In what ways does the image of God affect the way we treat others?

- How does the realization that the assignment of work by God change the perspective of our jobs?

Further Study

- Can you think of a time in your life when God's power and authority met with His gentleness and closeness? Why do you think God resting was mentioned, since He was finished?

- How does it impact you, knowing the God who made the heavens and Earth, chose to make you in His image?

- In what areas of your life do you feel that you reflect God the best? What areas do you feel you reflect Him the least?

- What do you think God's original plan for Adam was?

- What do you think the picture of Eden teaches us about sexuality and marriage? In what ways can we evaluate our relationships in view of God's original intentions?

Daily reading on Light

John 8;12, Psalm 119:105, John 12:35, Romans 13:11-14, Acts 13:47

Lesson 3 - The Fall Study Guide
Genesis 3:1-7, Genesis 6:11-18, Genesis 11:1-7

1. In all three stories, do you think God's judgment was too harsh? Why are we affected by the sins of another? How does the Gospel message of Jesus challenge our view of what's fair?

2. What were the distorted beliefs that led Adam and Eve to sin? How does doubt affect our prayer life?

3. How do God's love for His creation and love for His glory lead to grief over our rebellion? Why did they cover themselves up? Do we judge people's morals based on how they look? **Job 31:33, Isaiah 29:13**

4. God singled out Noah as righteous. How did Noah's family benefit from his relationship with God? How does your relationship with God affect your family?

5. What was wrong with the people of Babel unifying as one? God, Himself, said that together there would be nothing they couldn't do.

FURTHER STUDY

1. How does the reality of judgment affect our sense of urgency in proclaiming the Gospel?

2. How does **1 Peter 3:20-21** relate to Noah? In what ways are Noah and Jesus alike?

3. What downward spiral of consequences have you experienced as a result of sin? What does this experience tell us about sin?

4. How can we show the world that we desire God's recognition over man's recognition?

5. Look at some of the choices you have made in your life. In what ways do we doubt God's goodness? In what ways are we tempted to seek happiness outside of God?

Daily Verses on Doubt

Matt. 17:20, James 1:6-8, Joshua 1:9, 2 Chronicles 20:15-17, Romans 15:1-2

Lesson 4 - Abraham's Covenant
Gen 12:1-4, Gen 15, Gen 17:1-14

1. Abram was 75 when he left home. He had no children. How likely would it have seemed for God's promise for Abram to father a nation? Has there been a time in your life when God supplied you with a blessing that seemed impossible?

2. What can we tell about Abram's faith in Genesis 12:4? **James 2:14-26** Faith requires action. What are some ways your faith shows through in your daily life?

3. God's promise to Abram centered on him having a son. Without an heir, the continuation of Abram's family would be impossible. How did God's promise in **Genesis 3:15** relate to this promise?

4. In Chapter 15, several years had passed and Abram still had no son. How would you feel if you were in Abram's shoes at this time? What are some ways we can keep our faith strong when we feel God has stopped working in our lives?

5. How does Jesus relate to God's covenant with Abram?

Further Study

1. **Genesis 15:17-21.** The splitting of animals to finalize a covenant contract was a common business practice in Abram's time. The two parties making the deal would walk through the separated animals as a symbolic gesture showing that if one of them broke the covenant, he would surrender himself for slaughter like the animals. Knowing this, what is the significance of God walking through alone?

2. **Romans 4:1-4, 18-22** Why is this passage important concerning Abraham and the other saints of the Old Testament? Does this contradict **James 2:14-26?** Why or why not?

3. **Genesis 16:1-4** There is an old saying that goes, "You need to put shoes on your prayers," which means your prayers requires action. What is the difference in acting on faith and what Abram did with Sarai? Why is it difficult for us to trust God?

4. What was the purpose of circumcision? **Colossians 3:1-3** How does this passage relate to God's command of circumcision? How do we remain set apart and still fulfill our duty from question 9?

Daily reading on Faith in action
1 John 3:18, Luke 11:9-10, Collosians 3:2, Matthew 6:31-33, Psalm 146:6-8

Lesson 5- The Exodus
Exodus 6:2-9, Exodus 12:5-13, Exodus 14:10-14

1. Why did God rescue the Israelites from slavery? How does God's reminder of His Covenant with Abraham affect us today?

2. The Israelites had been in slavery for 400 years. How are we supposed to hold on to the promises God has made to us if we may never live to see them come to fruition

3. In Exodus 6:9, Moses tells the people about God's plan, but they didn't listen because their spirits were broken. Can you think of a time when you or someone you knew was so broken in spirit that the Gospel just seemed too good to be true? How would you help someone in that situation?

4. In Exodus 14:10-14, we have an example of how people can be taken out of slavery in an instant, but you cannot always take the slavery out of the person. What are some of the things that are hanging on in your life, which hurt your relationship with God that you just don't seem to be able to get rid of?

5. Who is the hero in this story? What are some similarities between Moses and Jesus?

Further Study

1. Are there things you are tempted to trust more than God for your safety, provision and comfort because God seems distant?

2. Have there been times in your life when God moved you out of your comfort zone and took you to difficult places to develop you? How has God shaped and empowered you even during times when He seemed absent?

3. What do you think God wanted to teach His people by sending a plague that would affect Hebrews and Egyptians alike? How does God's action reveal the universality of sin and our need for salvation?

4. In what ways does the biblical view of freedom differ from the world's? How is our mission as God's people influenced by seeing ourselves as freed to serve?

5. In what ways doe the complaining of the Israelites point a mirror to our own hearts? How does the tug of slavery to sin still affect our hearts even after we are redeemed?

Daily Reading - Freedom
Galatians 5:1, 2 Corinthians 3:17, John 8:36, Romans 8:15, Psalm 56:4

Lesson 6 – The Law
Exodus 34:1-9, Leviticus 19:1-2, Deuteronomy 6:4-5, Numbers 14:11-19

1. Look at the 10 Commandments. Are they a set of regulations we must abide by to have a relationship with God, or are they sign of His Grace and Glory? Why?

2. What does Exodus 34 show us about God's ability for forgiveness? Does verse 7 contradict this idea? Why?

3. Let's look at just the 10 Commandments. How many of just these 10 have you been able to uphold? Read **James 2:10**. How does this verse affect your understanding of the Law?

4. God is more interested in our love for Him, than our individual actions. Read **Deut. 6:5**. How does this passage speak to you? Now read **Matthew 22:34 – 40**. What does Jesus add? Does this change your understanding of the Old Testament Law? If so, how?

5. How is our mission to others affected when we align our hearts to God's heart for the world? Why is it true that those who love God will overflow with love for others?

FURTHER STUDY (See all 613 laws in Charts & Table Section)

6. In Exodus 34:5-6, why do you think God proclaimed His own name to Moses and the Israelites?

7. Read **Numbers 14:11-19**. What do you think kept God from destroying the Israelites at this point? Was it Moses ability to reason with God, or Moses' faith that God was who He said He was? What verses help support your answer?

8. Leviticus 19:1-2, God tells us we must be Holy if we are to have a relationship with Him. There were 613 laws that God ordained must be held at all times to be considered Holy. God set these laws to reinforce our need to have God's grace and mercy in our lives and that we are unable, without His help, to be worthy of a relationship with Him. Read **Matthew 5:17-20**. How does Jesus accomplish His goal?

9. We need someone in our lives to believe in God's faithfulness like Moses did for the Israelites. We need someone to believe when we don't. Jesus is that someone for us.

10. Read **Numbers 32:13** how does this relate to **Exodus 34:7**?

DAILY READING - FORGIVENESS
1 John 1:9, Isaiah 43:25, Ephesians 1:7, Colossians 1:13-14, Psalm 103:12
Lesson 7 -The Land

Joshua 1:1-9, Judges 2:11-19, Ruth 4:14-17

1. God does not make vague promises **(Genesis 15:18-21)**. What are the three promises God makes to Joshua?

2. Joshua had just been appointed to take over for Moses. He was about to lead 2 million people into a hostile and unknown land. God reassures Him by telling him to be courageous and strong. What does being courageous and strong look like in your life?

3. In Judges 2, what was the purpose of God raising judges for the Israelites? Who would you say play the roles of judges today?

4. What are some of the good gifts of God that people squander? How does our sin cheapen God's good gifts? (creation, sex, family, etc.)

5. In Ruth 4:14-17, who is the main character? How does this book reinforce God is a keeper of promises?

For Further Study

1. God promised to reconcile our relationship with Him **(Genesis 3:15)**. He promised to never leave us **(Joshua 1:5)**. He promised us rest with a light burden **(Matthew 11:28-29)**. He promised to never allow us to be tempted without way to get out **(1 Corinthians 10:13)**. He promised to come back for us **(John 14:3)**. Either we completely believe God and what He promises or we don't. What are some reasons you think make you distrust God?

2. What is the link between courage and disobedience to God? How does assurance of God's generosity and faithfulness lead us to be strong and courageous?

3. In what ways do we mimic the rebellious people of Israel? Both before and after Christ?

4. Read **Matthew 12:43-45.** How does this passage relate to Judges 2? What areas of your life has this passage been true?

5. Ruth was a foreigner, but because of her relationship with Naomi, God used her in His plan to fulfill His promise to Abraham. Who is looking at your relationship with God? What would they say about this relationship?

DAILY READING - COURAGE
1 Corinthians 15:58, Ephesians 6:10, John 14:27, 2 Timothy 1:7, Proverbs 3:5-6

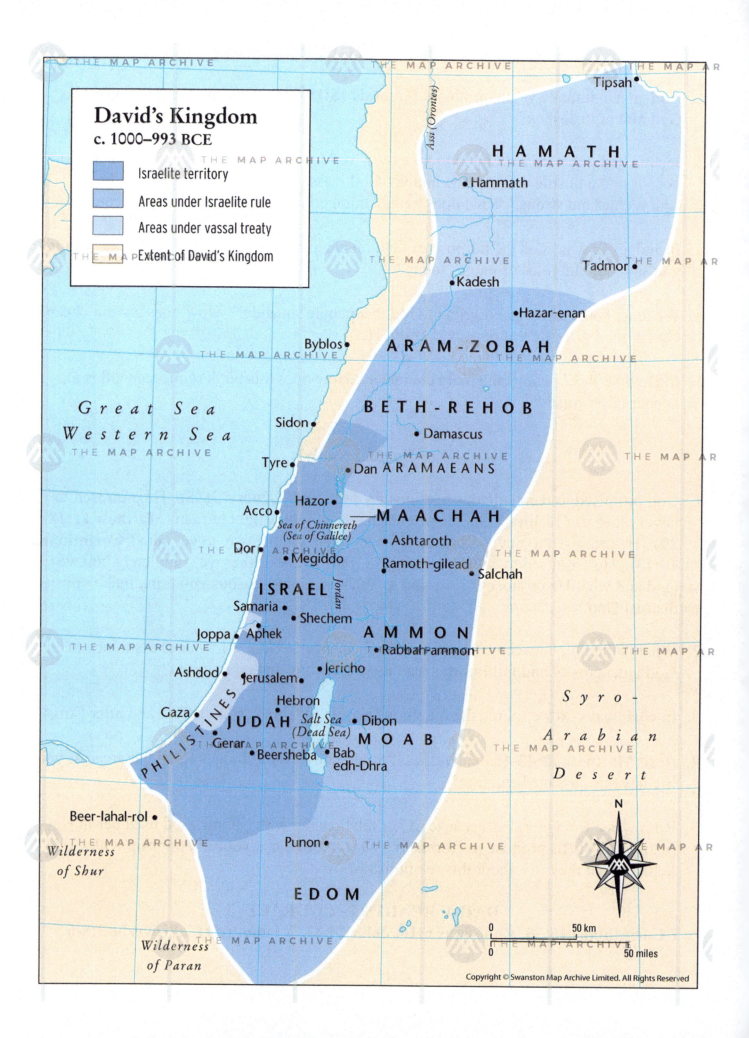

Lesson 8 - The Kings (Deuteronomy 17:14-20)
1 Samuel 8:1-9, 2 Samuel 7:10-24, 1 Kings 8:54-61

1. Read **Genesis 2:15**. How does this passage relate to David in **2 Samuel 7:11-16**? What role did David play to the Israelites? What role did David play for God? What are some areas in your life that God has put you in charge of?

2. In **2 Samuel 7:14**, why does God use the father/son reference when speaking about David's son? What is your relationship with your Heavenly father like? What traits or lessons have you learned from Him that affects your life today?

3. In **2 Samuel 7:18-24**, David gives thanks to God for showing Favor on the Israelites. These people were not unique to God for any qualities of their own, only that they were chosen by God. Read **1 Corinthians 1:26-31.** What are some ways we can show God how grateful we are for what He has done in our lives?

4. In **1 Kings 8:57-58,** why do you think Solomon prayed for God to cause us to follow and obey His commands? Aren't we responsible to obey regardless? How does his example of prayer in verse 58 affect our prayer life?

5. The nations around Israel were to know there was no other God, but God, by the way Israel lived their lives. What does this teach us about the local church and its evangelism? How can we personally help our church's evangelism?

Further Study

- Read **1 Samuel 8:4-9**. Why did the people want a king?(v. 5) God had guided Israel with men, known as Judges up until this point. What are some reasons you think the people would want a king over a religious leader? How are most religious leaders looked at today? Do you think we would be better off as a country with a religious leader or a president? Why?

- In **2 Samuel 7:11-16,** we see that everything David had came from God and everything that was promised would come from God. Yet, who gets the credit for David's victories? What are some successes in your life that you wrongly took credit for? Read **1 Corinthians 4:7.** How does this affect the way we should look at the successes in our lives?

- Up until 2 Samuel 7:16 we assumed God was talking about David's son, Solomon, but we see here that God is alluding to someone else. Forever is a long time. Jesus was both a son to David and to God who fulfilled this promise. Jesus' full right as king on Earth came from David, while His authority over all Creation came from His Heavenly Father.

- God said that He redeemed Israel to make a great name for Himself. How is God making a great name for Himself through your life? What ways do you try to steal fame from God? What ways do you shape your life to promote God's name?

- Solomon was known as the wisest man in all the Earth, yet with even all His wisdom, he was unable to stay on the mountain top. Soon, everything he had accomplished would be undone and lost. We need a deeper wisdom that will bring peace and harmony to our lives. Read **1 Corinthians 1: 22-24.** Where can we find this wisdom?

Daily Reading - God's Promises
Jeremiah 29:11, Philippians 4:19, Romans 8:37-39, John 14:27, John 3:16-18

United Kingdom				
Years (BC)	King	Start / End	Prophet	Scripture
1050 - 1010	Saul	Good / Evil	Samuel	1 Sa 8-31 1 Ch 9-10
1010 - 970	David (Captain)	Good / Good	Samuel Nathan	1 Sa 16-31 2 Sa 1-24 1 Ki 1-2 1 Ch 11-29
970 - 930	Solomon (Son)	Good / Evil	Nathan	1 Ki 1-11 2 Ch 1-9

Divided Kingdom

	Judah					Israel			
Years	King	Start / End	Prophet	Scripture	Years	King	Start / End	Prophet	Scripture
931 - 913	Rehoboam (Son)	Evil / Evil	Shemaiah	1 Ki 12, 14 2 Ch 10-12	931 - 910	Jeroboam I (servant)	Evil / Evil	Ahijah	1 Ki 12-14 2 Ch 10
913 - 911	Abijah (Son)	Evil / Evil		1 Ki 15 2 Ch 13					
911 - 870	Asa (Son)	Good/Good	Hanani	1 Ki 15 2 Ch 14-16	910 - 909	Nadab (son)	Evil / Evil		1 Ki 15
					909 - 886	Baasha	Evil / Evil	Jehu	1 Ki 16
					886 - 885	Elah (Son)	Evil / Evil		1 Ki 16
					885	Zimri (Captain)	Evil / Evil	Micaiah	1 Ki 16
					885 - 874	Omri (Captain)	Evil / Evil	Elijah 1 Ki 17-19 1 Ki 21 2 Ki 1-2	1 Ki 16
					874 - 853	Ahab (Son)	Evil / Evil		1 Ki 17 2 Ch 18
870 - 848	Jehoshaphat (Son)	Good/Good		1 Ki 22 2 Ch 17-20	853 - 852	Ahaziah (Son)	Evil / Evil		1 Ki 22 2 Ki 1
848 - 841	Jehoram (Son)	Evil / Evil	Obadiah(?)	2 Ki 8 2 Ch 21	852 - 841	Joram (Son of Ahab)	Evil / Evil	Elisha 1 Ki 19 2 Ki 2-9 2 Ki 13	2 Ki 3
841	Ahaziah (Son)	Evil / Evil		2 Ki 8-9 2 Ch 22	841 - 814	Jehu (Captain)	Good / Evil		2 Ki 9-10
841 - 835	Athaliah (mother)	Evil / Evil		2 Ki 11 2 Ch 22-23					
835 - 796	Joash (son of Ahaziah)	Good / Evil	Joel	2 Ki 11-12 2 Ch 23-24	814 - 798	Jehoahaz (Son)	Evil / Evil		2 Ki 13
796 - 767	Amaziah (son)	Good / Evil		2 Ki 14 2 Ch 25	798 - 782	Jehoash (Son)	Evil / Evil		2 Ki 13-14
					782 - 753	Jeroboam II (Son)	Evil / Evil		2 Ki 14
767 - 740	Uzziah aka Azariah (Son)	Good/Evil	Isaiah Micah	2 Ki 15 2 Ch 26	753 - 752	Zechariah (Son)	Evil / Evil	Amos Hosea Jonah (2 Kings 14:25; Jonah 1:1) Micah	2 Ki 15
					752	Shallum	Evil / Evil		2 Ki 15
					752 - 742	Menahem	Evil / Evil		2 Ki 15
					742 - 740	Pekahiah (Son)	Evil / Evil		2 Ki 15
748 - 732	Jotham (Son)	Good/Good		2 Ki 15 2 Ch 27	752 - 740 (rival) 733 - 722 (sole)	Pekah (Captain)	Evil / Evil		2 Ki 15
732 - 716	Ahaz (Son)	Evil / Evil		2 Ki 16 2 Ch 28 Is 7	732 - 722	Hoshea	Evil / Evil		2 Ki 17
716 - 687	Hezekiah (Son)	Good/Good		2 Ki 18-20 2 Ch 29-32 Is 36-39	**Israel into Assyrian captivity - 722 BC**				
687 - 642	Manasseh (Son)	Evil / Good		2 Ki 21 2 Ch 33				Nahum	
642 - 640	Amon (Son)	Evil / Evil		2 Ki 21 2 Ch 33					
640 - 608	Josiah (Son)	Good/Good		2 Ki 22-23 2 Ch 34-35					
608	Jehoahaz (Son)	Evil / Evil		2 Ki 23 2 Ch 36				Daniel	
608 - 597	Jehoiakim (Son of Josiah)	Evil / Evil	Habakkuk Zephaniah Jeremiah Ezekiel (Lamentations)	2 Ki 23-24 2 Ch 36					
597	Jehoiachin (Son)	Evil / Evil		2 Ki 24-25 2 Ch 36					
597 - 586	Zedekiah (Son of Josiah)	Evil / Evil		2 Ki 24-25 2 Ch 36					
Judah into Babylonian captivity - 586 BC									
586-450			Jeremiah Haggai Zechariah Malachi						

Lesson 9 - Psalms and Wisdom
Psalm 1:1-6, Psalm 51:1-6, Proverbs 1:7, Job 1:20-21, Ecclesiastes 12:13-14

1. Do you have a favorite song at church? Does it help you become more spirited or promote a feeling that you are closer to God? What is it about this song that gives you this feeling?

2. How does the knowledge that we cannot fully live according to the wise path we read about in Psalm 1 drive us to the Gospel?

3. What are some excuses we use to justify our sins? In what ways do we seek to blame others for our sins?

4. How do you define wisdom? What characteristics define a "wise" person? How does the Bible define Wisdom? What was Job's understanding of wisdom?

5. How is fear of judgment one of the ways God keeps us from making sinful choices or living with misguided priorities?

FURTHER STUDY

1. What do the songs we sing say about who we are and what we value? What songs does your heart naturally sing? What songs do you and those around you sing?

2. How can we, as a body of believers, challenge one another to be more open to quick confession of sin? Why is it important to have confession to God before we offer confession to others? In what ways can we share the mercy shown to us with others?

3. What comes to mind when you think of "fear of the Lord"? Is this the same as being afraid of God? Why?

4. Can love ever be foolish and wrong? When? Under what circumstances?

5. Proverbs is a wise guide for moral principles. Ecclesiastes and Job are examples of wisdom applied in the harsh realities of life. Sometimes, there seem to be discrepancies between principles and reality. How would you explain these discrepancies to someone?

Daily Reading - Worship and Wisdom
Proverbs 3:5, Psalm 119:105, Proverbs 4:23, Psalm 1:1, Proverbs 27:17

Lesson 10 - Israel
1 Kings 18:20-39, 2 Kings 17:6-18

1. Elijah seemed to be the lone advocate for God. The people of Israel were God's chosen people, it was part of their heritage as well as their religion, yet they were worshiping a false God. In **1 Kings 18:21** Elijah told the people to chose one, yet there was no answer from the people. How can our hesitation to give God our worship point to possible idols in our lives? What are some practical ways we can overcome our hesitation?

2. If Elijah believed that God would consume the sacrifice with fire, why did he step toward the altar (18:36)? If he really believed that God would act, shouldn't he have stepped away from it? What kind of clue does this give us about God's majestic yet gracious character?

3. What are some ways we can keep our hearts from drifting to other gods (things that come between us and God)? How does the good news that God accepts us through the work of Jesus affect our ability to put God before any idol? What are some ways we can strengthen our resolve against idols?

4. What effects does one generation have on the next? What traits are we passing down to the next generation of believers?

5. How does the knowledge that we become like what we worship encourage us to be more faithful in our worship of Jesus?

Further study

1. Why does God take Idolatry so seriously? What is at stake when we allow something to come between our worship to God? Read **1 Corinthians 10:14.** What verb does Paul use? What does this say about how we should deal with idolatry in our lives?

2. In what ways does Elijah's prayer model the way we should pray for God to work in our lives? Would you be willing to risk you reputation to God if it would bring Him greater glory?

3. Think about God's work in your own life. What are some lessons that you have learned from the spiritual valleys you have gone through? In what ways does God's influence on your past reflect on your life today?

4. The Israelites secretly sinned against God (**2 Kings 17:9**). What secret sins or habits do you have that take precedence over your love for God?

5. How does our distinctiveness aid us in our mission as God's people?

Daily Reading - Worship
Psalm 100:4, Psalm 59:16, John 4:24, 1 Chronicles 16:34, Romans 14:11

Lesson 11 - Judah
Isaiah 6:8-13, Jeremiah 31:31-34, 2 Chronicles 36:15-21

1. How does Isaiah's commission influence the way we look at our call to evangelize? **(Isaiah 6:8)** How does understanding God's role in salvation free us to focus on being faithful witnesses who entrust the results to Him?

2. God called Isaiah to deliver a message of judgment. He had a choice. Either deliver a message the people would want to hear, or be faithful to God and remaining obedient. Read **John 3:27 & 30.** How does this apply to your life of being popular or obedient?

3. In Jeremiah 31:34, God says He will remember their sin no more. Read **1 Corinthians 13:7.** Is this characteristic of love present in your life? In what ways does God's forgiveness for you help you to forget the sins committed against you?

4. Why is it easy for us to go through the motions of Christianity without truly allowing God to change us? What are the dangers of this type of lifestyle? **(Mathew 7:21-23)**

5. How does God's judgment shine light on His character? How does God's mercy show His character? Do these two contradict each other? Why or why not?

FURTHER STUDY

1. Throughout the Old Testament, a prophet was considered to be the mouthpiece of God. Read **Isaiah 51:36.** While God put words in Isaiah's mouth, what is the danger of us putting words in God's mouth?

2. In what ways have you chosen faithfulness over worldly success? Can God uses successes in our lives to accomplish His will? If so, how?

3. Do you really believe that God is capable of forgetting anything? What does **Hebrews 8:12** mean? What effect should this have on our sanctification?

4. When we eat at a good restaurant, or see a good movie, we share the experience with our friends so they can experience the pleasure as well. This is called being a witness. Do you do the same thing with your experiences with God? How should God's righteous love inspire our witness to others?

5. The Southern Kingdom's situation was bad, but never hopeless. How did God bring hope through judgment? Read **1 Peter 1:3.** What kind of living hope is Peter talking about? How has this hope helped you get through some seemingly hopeless times in your life?

Daily Reading - Called to serve
John 12:26, Matthew 6:24, Romans 12:1, Malachi 3:17-18, Ephesians 2:10

Lesson 12 - The Exile
Daniel 1:8-17, Ezekiel 37:1-14

1. Why does God insist on being faithful to the covenant He established, even though His people continue to be unfaithful? Read **Matthew 5:17-20.** The covenant changed with Jesus to include everyone. Is there evidence of this covenant today? If so, how?

2. God had given the Israelites specific rules about foods that were unclean to eat (Deuteronomy 14, Leviticus 11). By requesting special food, Daniel not only put his own life in danger by defying the king, but he put the guard's life in danger as well. What was the compromise that Daniel proposed to the guard? Think about the last decision you made based on your faith. Did it have consequences? If so, what were they?

3. Daniel and his friends were handpicked for their looks and their intelligence by the king to learn the ways of Babylon, in hopes they would spread the kingdom's influence on the other Jews. In verse 17, we are told their knowledge and understanding came from God. What areas of our lives do we mistakenly take credit for as accomplishing on our own, when we should be thanking God for the blessing?

4. Why is it important to notice in Ezekiel 37, that the life of the bones came from the word of God? Read **2 Timothy 3:16.** How does this passage suggest we should view scripture?

5. How are people restricted by sin? How does our salvation make it possible to overcome these restrictions?

Further Study

1. Daniel found himself in a foreign country surrounded by a culture that did not believe or honor God. We often find ourselves in a similar situation right now in our own country. How does God's faithfulness to Daniel inspire you to remain faithful?

2. How can you demonstrate the truth of the Gospel in ways that are understood to the world even though they are radically different from its values?

3. In what ways does the promise of resurrection change your view of death? Your view of life? What is the connection between converted hearts and sharing the good news of Jesus?

4. Read **Luke 9:23.** The cross represents death. Why is it important for Christians to approach death with faith and confidence rather that fear and doubt?. How do you die daily?

5. Read **John 5:24.** Do you know someone who has not yet "passed from death to life"? In what ways is God using you to reach that person? What is the greatest barrier to their salvation?

Daily Readings - Faithful to God
1 Kings 2:3-4, Ephesians 5:22-25, 1 Peter 4:19, Deuteronomy 11:13, Deuteronomy 29:9

Lesson 13 - The Return
Ezra 3:10-13, Zechariah 8:1-8

1. Read **Revelation 21:22.** John says, "I did not see the sanctuary in it." How does he finish his statement? What is the importance of living in a temple-less Jerusalem?

2. How does God's promise of future restoration give us hope in our present realities? In what ways does God's promise urge us into action?

3. What is the connection between the power of God and the jealousy of God? Why is God's Jealousy good news for His people? How does the knowledge of God's jealousy inspire us to be ministers of reconciliation?

4. What can the memory of your past teach you about what God requires of your future?

5. In Malachi 4, God promises reconciliation with His people. Because of Jesus, when we are saved, we become God's adopted children. How can show our dissatisfaction with the current world, while retaining the hope that God to reconcile everyone to Him?

FURTHER STUDIES

1. We have all have high expectations at one time or another that we became disappointed in, when they did not come to fruition. How can times of disappointment like this bring a sense of joy that only God can give?

2. What does it mean to be a redeemed person in an unrestored world? In what ways should this joyful mourning be the expression of every Christian?

3. Read **Revelation 21:1-3** in conjunction with **Zech. 8:1-8**. What are some spiritual disciplines that make us anxious for the new Heaven and new Earth? (**Galatians 5:22-23** for example)

4. Why is it difficult, many times, to live in light of the promise of God's presence and His promises? How does modern culture and the media depict those who live with hope in God's promised future?

5. Read **Ezra 1:1-4.** Like King Cyrus' decree, how God's Word free us to live in peace with others while also preparing for future restoration? If Scripture is one long story, what would you say its primary theme would be? How do you fit into the story?

Daily Reading - Restoration
1 Peter 5:10, Psalm 71:20, Romans 12:2, Titus 3:5, Isaiah 61:7

Lesson 14 - The New Testament Introduction

- **400 years between OT and NT**
- **Political standings**
    - Conquest of Alexander the Great unified the area into Roman city state, Greek is common language, Oppression of Jews
    - Sadducees are Roman appointed officials used to keep Jews in line
    - Pharisees are believers and keepers of the Law, Jewish scholars
    - Herod the Great rebuilt the temple in Jerusalem to appease the people
    - Temple and Synagogue
- **The Gospels**
    - 4 views of Christ divided into Synoptic (Matt., Mark, Luke) and Gospel of John
    - MATTHEW – Mary -focus on Jesus as rightful Messianic King come to fulfill the Old Testament prophecies, Genealogy from Abraham (include women and imperfections), 3 groups of 14 generations (7 is perfect number, 3 represents truthful witness). Many references to the OT. Was written to the Jews. Author is traditionally known as the tax collector apostle Matthew. Book written approx. late 70's – early 80s.
    - MARK – Focus on Jesus as the servant son of God. Written to the Romans, early converts. No genealogy. Written late 60's – early 70's. Author traditionally John Mark of Jerusalem (Acts 12:12, 15:37). Shortest Gospel.
    - LUKE – Focus on Jesus as the perfect man. Joseph Genealogy from Adam. (Men only) Author conscripted by Theophilus, educated physician also wrote book of Acts (investigative reporting). Written to the Gentiles. Written in mid 80s.
    - JOHN – Focus on Jesus as eternal God whose sacrifice we gain eternal life. Traditionally written by Apostle John. Written main addition 90s, with early writings as soon as 50s. Written to everyone.
- **Manuscripts** – 5,000+ (2.6 million pages) original Greek, 10,000 Latin and 9,000 additional Syrian, Coptic and Aramaic. All written by 100 AD.
    - Discrepancies in translations (16 missing verses from NIV). All hand written. Possible notations added by scribes. Collections from Egypt and Rome
    - Formal, functional, paraphrase – No English translations for Greek words
- **Canon**
    - Old Testament – 200BC (approx)
        - Hebrew OT contains 24 books. Same material divided into 39 books for Christians. Catholic Bible contains more OT books, based on the Septuagint (Greek translation of Hebrew scripture).

- New Testament set in mid 4th century Codex Sinaiticus (*c.* 350) (no one group or church decided. Out of need to uncover heretical material ie. Gospel of Mary, Gospel of Thomas, the Apocalypse of Peter.)
  - Chapters and verses were not added until 16th century.
  - **English translations John Wycliffe – 1384 (3-4 people using primarily Vulgate), King James 1611 (50 scholars using Greek manuscripts and Wycliffe translation. 84% came from Wycliffe).**

Lesson – 15 - The Incarnation
John 1:1-18

1. What are some of the similarities in the opening of John's Gospel and the opening of Genesis? Jesus is often referred to as the second Adam. **1 Corinthians 15:21-22, 45-49** What attributes do Adam and Jesus share?

2. Darkness is the absence of light. Light is not the absence of darkness, but is a presence that repels darkness. In verse 5, what is the light that shines in the darkness (**John 8:12**)? How can the hope of this light repel the darkness in our lives?

3. **John 1:6-8** What comes to mind when you hear the word "witnessing"? Greek core word "Martys" meaning Martyr. Most of the time in the New Testament, Witness means to attest to facts or confirms the truth of something. **Luke 9:23** How does this alter or change your view of being a witness? What is the main focus of John's witness?

4. What, in your personal testimony, shows how God's power changed your life? What is easier for you to do, witness for Jesus or share your testimony? Why?

5. In verses 17-18, the invisible God of the Old Testament is now visible to us. How is God's grace and glory of the Old Testament strengthened and fulfilled in Jesus?

FURTHER STUDY

1. How do you think most non-believers view God and what He is like? How did you view God before you were saved? How does Jesus those expectations of what God is like? How are they different?

2. What does it take for you to have confidence and trust someone? Based on what John says in verses 1-5 about the Word, can you have confidence in Him? Why?

3. Why do you think that the creator of the universe needed a witness? Does He need less of a witness today? If you could only say one sentence to someone about Jesus, what would it be?

4. When was the "but now" moment in your life? How was God's power evident in saving and changing your life? How does your life before Christ compare to your life now?

5. How does your reflection of God's grace help us bear witness to Him? How is our relationship with Jesus different from the people of the Old Testament? How is it the same?

Lesson 16 - Jesus' Teachings
Mark 1:14-15, Luke 4:16-21, Luke 8:4-8, Matthew 7:28-29

1. What do you think of when you hear the term "Kingdom of God"? Jesus' greatness didn't come from His successes; it came from who He was. He didn't have to be appointed king; His authority came from who He was as the creator of the universe. Why do you think Jesus speaks of the kingdom's arrival as "good news"?

2. In what ways has Jesus' authority over your life caused you to change your worldly agendas for His kingdom ones? Why is it import that repentance and faith be seen as more than a one time event?

3. The seed Jesus used in His parable was the Word of God. How does this parable help you to understand the storyline and purpose of all scripture? In what ways are you actively "sowing the seed" of the Gospel?

4. What are some practical ways Christians can more knowledgeable about the Word of God? What role does faith play in reading scripture? **1 Corinthians 2:14**

5. What are some ways Christians fall short of living under Jesus' authority? What are some things that we just write of as only something Jesus could do and not even try?

Further Study

1. In what ways should our lives show the saving power of God's kingdom? How does Christ's authority come through in our lives in a way that others can see, without us having to tell them we are Christians?

2. Think about some of your greatest achievements. How many of them did you complete all on your own? How do you compare our need for others to Jesus, who set a vision Himself and then accomplished it without the need of anyone else.

3. In what ways can we enjoy life under the rule of King Jesus even when we are living in a broken world? How does the church point to the day when God's Kingdom will come in its fullness?

4. Does the audience's reaction in Matthew 7 relate to your own story in any way? If so, how? How does this influence the way you witness to family and friends who do not know Christ?

5. How do you live your life in such a way that God's kingdom agenda mission is obvious?

Further Reading - Kingdom of God
Psalm 47:7-8, Mark 11:10, Daniel 7:14, Luke 17:20-21, Psalm 9:7-8

Lesson 17 - Jesus' Miracles
Mark 1:29-34, John 6:1-15, Luke 7:18-28

1. Sickness is a result of the fall. God never intended us to be sick or to even die, but Adam and Eve's disobedience introduced death and disease to the world. How does Jesus' work reverse the effects of the fall? What are some physical ways we see Jesus still working to reverse the consequences of the fall in our world today?

2. Why is worship and service (ministry) a natural response to our salvation? How do our actions show others that Jesus is alive and here among us?

3. A consumer is someone who always takes and is concerned mostly about themselves. What is the difference between a consumer in church and a worshiper? How can recognizing the difference help us to be better worshipers?

4. The people on the mountain wanted Jesus' power and what he could give them, but they didn't want to accept His authority (**John 6:14-15**). How do we balance helping the needy but make sure they understand Jesus is Lord?

5. What does it look like to be an ambassador for the Kingdom of God? How can Jesus' demonstration of the power of the Kingdom of God, through His miracles, give us encouragement to share the gospel?

Further Study

1. What are some areas of your life that have been affected by the fall? How would your life be different if suddenly the world was changed back to the way God intended it to be?

2. How does your life reflect the compassion of Jesus? How did someone else's compassion for Jesus lead you to follow Him? How can we make sure that the love of Jesus is our motivation for ministering to others and doing good deeds?

3. In **John,** if Jesus already knew what He was going to do, why do you thing He asked the disciples what to do? What did they're answer say about their faith? Have you ever been tested by Jesus in your life? Why is it so hard for us to trust that Jesus will follow through in our lives?

4. Has there been a time in your life when God scattered your expectations? How should we deal with disappointment when God's plan does not match up to our plans and expectations? How would help a disappointed Christian through a time when they question God's goodness?

Lesson 18 - The Cross
Matthew 16:13-24, Matthew 26:26-29, Matthew 27:45-50

1. People misunderstood who Jesus was and His ministry 2000 years ago. What are some of the misconceptions people have about Jesus and His ministry today? Why is it important to understand what people think about Jesus? How have you come to your understanding of who Jesus is?

2. What are some ways people try to mold Jesus to suit their purpose? How central is the cross to your understanding of who Jesus is? In what ways is taking up the cross connected to following Jesus and His mission?

3. What might be some reasons for the Passover celebration being the time for Jesus' suffering and death? In what ways was the Passover event a picture pointing toward Christ? (Read **Exodus 12:1-30** to understand Passover)

4. God brought redemption to us out of the darkest of days when Jesus died. He is also working to bring good out of the suffering we go through (**Romans 8:28**). How does the cross provide comfort during these trials?

5. Christ suffered and sacrificed Himself for us. How does His sacrifice urge us to sacrifice our comfort in order to reach others with the good news of forgiveness?

Further Study

1. Have you ever been in a situation where people misunderstood your intentions? What did you do to correct that misunderstanding?

2. Describe a time when you had to pay the cost for following Jesus (financially, socially or a friendship)

3. The old covenant God had with His people required regular sacrifices to cover their sins. How does His new covenant through Christ differ? How does this new covenant produce joy and peace for you?

4. Jesus knew He would have to suffer for our sins. So why do you think He asked God why He had forsaken Him?

5. What do we learn about our salvation from Jesus' last words on the cross (**Matt. 27:46, Luke 23:46, John 19:30**)? How do these words strengthen your faith? Which passage holds the most meaning to you? Why?

Lesson 19 - The Resurrection
Luke 24: 1-53

1. In what ways does Christ's resurrection represent a *new beginning,* rather than a *happy ending?* Why is this understanding important?

2. How did the disciples respond to Jesus' resurrection? How did it affect their view of Him and His work? How does the resurrection affect our understanding of Jesus and His work?

3. How did Jesus deal with the disciple's disbelief (v. 37-41)? What are some ways to overcome our doubts in Jesus? What difference does it make when Jesus still approaches us, even in our doubt?

4. How does Christ's patience with the disciples encourage us as we help others in various stages of their spiritual walk?

5. How are the different areas of our lives (work, family, recreation, government) affected by the knowledge that Jesus reigns over all?

Further Study

1. What are some resurrection themes you've seen in movies or books? What about in nature? How do they compare to Jesus' resurrection?

2. What do the emotions of awe, wonder, and joy play in your sharing of the good news of Jesus' death and resurrection with others?

3. What hope does Christ's resurrection give us when we are facing death? What others areas of your life are affected by His resurrection?

4. Jesus connected His death, resurrection and mission of the church to the Old Testament prophecies. He fulfilled 353 prophecies given about Him and His work in the Old Testament. How does this reinforce the promises He made to us about salvation, everlasting life and His coming back?

5. Why do you think the church doesn't give much attention to Jesus' ascension into Heaven? Why was His ascension the turning point in the disciple's mission? How does His ascension affect the church today?

Lesson 20 - Pentecost
Acts 2:1-47

1. In what ways do you think the church reflects God's heart with His promise to build people up? Why is it important for churches not to be guided by worldly culture when sharing and celebrating the gospel?

2. Why is it important for Christians to make the gospel accessible and understandable to non-believers? What are some examples you have used or seen that help make the Bible and God's message more relatable?

3. Sharing the gospel is one of the hardest things for most Christians to do. Is our lack of confidence in sharing the gospel due to our lack of faith in the power of the Spirit, or is it something else? If it is something else, what? Why is it important to recognize the supernatural aspect of salvation?

4. Why do you think it is important to emphasize baptism and church membership as part of being Christian? What are the dangers of being a church-less Christian?

5. Why is it important for churches to pray? Does group prayer increase or decrease our reliance on the Holy Spirit? How?

Further Study

1. Have you ever been discouraged at how difficult it is to follow Jesus sometimes? How do you deal with those times in your life? Think of a time when you tired to do something on your own and finally had to give in and leave it to God. What did you learn from that experience?

2. How does the presence of the Holy Spirit, in your life, affect your view of Christian living? How would describe the Spirit working in your life to someone else? Has the Spirit ever reminded you of a Bible verse at an important moment of decision when talking to someone else?

3. Peter does an excellent job of relaying the gospel in Act 2 to others. How would you explain the concepts of repentance and faith to someone who has never been to church or knows nothing about the Bible?

4. Has there ever been a time in your life when you were struggling with something and you just happened to be at the right place at the right time for someone to help you out? Why is community so important to Christians?

5. Do you think our church is similar to the church noted in Verses 41-47? What could you do to help make our church more like the early church?

Lesson 21 – Our Identity
Acts 15:1-5, Galatians 2:15-21, James 2:18-26

1. Why is the idea of Christ *plus* something else dangerous? In what ways does adding to salvation take the focus off of Jesus and lessen His Glory? How would you describe grace to a non believer?

2. How does the Jerusalem council emphasis on faith alone for salvation impact our mission to share the Gospel to all kinds of people?

3. In the Old Testament, God gave his people 613 laws in order to live righteously. He gave them, knowing no one would be able to live up to them all, but to reinforce the people's need for God, since He is the only one who is truly righteous. How does understanding the purpose of the law change the way we read and accept it?

4. What is the difference in saving faith and simply the knowledge of who Jesus was? (**James 2:19**). Why is it so important for saving faith to produce good works?

5. Read **Romans 3:27 – 4:5** and compare it to **James 2:15-21.** Do these passages contradict each other? Why or why not? How do our works affect our ability to share the Gospel?

FURTHER STUDY

1. Why do we expect to be treated fairly and graciously at the same time? What does this tell us about our hearts and how we view ourselves?

2. What are some unnecessary boundaries that churches put up concerning repentance? Is there anything in our church that you think may trip up a non believer from coming to Jesus? If so, what?

3. If God has shown us grace through Jesus, how should that affect our interactions with others? In what ways do you struggle with showing and receiving grace?

4. Is it possible to have assurance of salvation without producing any fruit of the spirit?

5. How does justification through faith alone free us to love our neighbors without seeking a reward?

Lesson 22 - Our Mission
1 Corinthians 1:18-25, 2 Corinthians 5:14-21, Philippians 2:1-4

1. What seems "foolish" or "offensive" about Christ's death and resurrection? What are some ways we may play down the foolishness or offensive nature of the gospel in order to make it fit with our culture?

2. What happens when we are compelled by something other than love in our involvement with God's mission?

3. What is an ambassador? In what ways should our lives reflect the priorities of an ambassador to the Kingdom of God? How do you convince someone of a home you've never seen for yourself?

4. Put yourself in Paul's chains while he wrote **Philippians 2**. If you were writing from prison, to Christians you knew and loved, what would you want them to know? What would your focus be?

5. Is unity the same thing as uniformity? How can Christians in a church learn to disagree well?

Further Study

1. How can our churches uphold and prioritize the gospel message as being of first importance? How does your presentation of the gospel compare to Paul's in **1 Corinthians 1:18-25**?

2. What resources do your church have that can be used for God's global mission? What are some ways you can get involved in God's global mission?

3. In what ways could you be tempted to trade our mission for a life of conformity to the world around us? What happens when we only focus on the benefits of salvation and not our calling from Jesus?

4. What are some examples of unity that comes from having a shared mission? The church is supposed to be active in missions as a community, not just as individuals. How can a church fulfill the mission of God as a community?

5. Have you ever seen rivalry and conceit within the church? If so, how did it affect the rest of the church? What are some ways you can promote unity within your church?

Lesson 23 - Justification
Romans 5:1, 12-21, Romans 8:1-2, Hebrews 9:11-14

1. At the end of the movie "Saving Private Ryan", the private stands before the captain who sacrificed his life for Ryan and says, "I hope I have earned the life you sacrificed for me." How is his response to his captain's sacrifice different from the Christian's response to Christ's sacrifice?

2. Why is sin related to death? What are the consequences of sin in relationships to others? **(Romans 6:21-23)**

3. How does the understanding that we are spiritually dead away from Christ, affect our prayers for those who do not know Him?

4. Jesus is often called the second Adam. How does Paul compare Jesus and Adam in **Romans 5:12-21?**

5. How was Christ's sacrifice permanent and continuously effective? How does our service to God demonstrate our faith in Christ's atonement?

Further Study

1. What is it about human nature that makes us try to "earn" the rewards that come from Jesus' sacrifice?

2. What are some of the signs in the world around us that sin and death have spread to all mankind since the fall of Adam?

3. How does your view of God change when you consider the fact that God's Son became a man, not only to be our mediator, but also our sacrifice? How is this different from other religions?

4. How does your understanding of the gospel impact your perspective on living out the Christian life in yourself and others?

5. In **Hebrews 9:14,** it mentions cleansing your conscience of dead works. What are dead works? How has your relationship with Christ changed a specific area of your life that would have been considered dead work in your past?

Lesson 24 - Following
1 Timothy 4:11-16, 2 Timothy 4:1-8, Titus 2:11-14

1. Timothy was a young follower of Christ that Paul took under his wing. **Read 1 Peter 5:2-5.** What are some examples of "little sheep" that God has entrusted to us? What are some ways we can be a good shepherd to them?

2. What do you think was Paul's main message to Timothy in **1 Timothy 4**? Have you ever gotten encouragement when your faith seemed to be failing? If so, who gave it to you and how did that affect your relationship with that person?

3. Is Paul's charge to Timothy in **2 Timothy 4:1-8** relevant today? How? If Paul were writing this letter to you, what would be some of the things you think he would encourage you to do?

4. Would you feel comfortable telling someone "watch me, and follow me as I follow Christ"? Why or Why not? What would you have to change for you to be comfortable showing others what it looks like to follow Jesus?

5. Can you give an example of an area where it might be easier for a church to follow a cultural trend rather than stand firm for the truth of God?

Further Study

1. What view of pastors changes for you, when you realize they are God's shepherds? What are the responsibilities of a shepherd? How can a church affirm the shepherding gifts of those God sets apart for pastoral ministry?

2. Describe a time when you were impacted by another Christian who proclaimed the truth and lived it out. How did their example impact the way you live out your faith today?

3. Can you think of a time it was costly for a pastor to preach the truth? How can we encourage a pastor to remain faithful with his messages?

4. In what ways does your life reflect or deny your eternal hope? What are some things God may be calling you to leave behind in order to join with Him in His ministry to reach lost sheep?

5. How does Christ's return affect out evangelistic efforts?

Lesson 25 - Perseverance
1 Peter 1:3-9, 2 Peter 3:8-13, 1 John 2:15-17

1. Why are we often inspired by stories of underdogs? In what ways do trials and hardship increase our joy when we are victorious?

2. Read **Roman 8:28.** How can Paul confidently claim that God is working all things together for the good of the believer? What kind of perspective supports this statement?

3. How does joyfulness in times of suffering show the rest of the world that Christ is to be treasured above everything else? How does reorienting our suffering around Christ's glory help us through trials?

4. How does our understanding that people live forever – either in Heaven or Hell – influence the way we look at others? How does this truth lead us to mission?

5. How can a Christian persevere against the lust of the flesh, the lust of the eyes, and the pride in one's lifestyle?

Further Study

1. When was the last time you suffered because of your faith? How did you respond to that trial? How did God use that trial to glorify Himself and mold you into the image of Christ?

2. How should **1 John 2:19** inform the way we relate to other believers?

3. In what ways does our future hope give us hope in times of trial? What are some ways we can focus on eternity in order to persevere today?

4. In your life, what are some ways that saying yes to the will of God will result in inward struggle or persecution from the world? How is our perseverance a witness to the world?

5. How would you respond to someone who says they would not come to your church because of the way someone in your church acts outside the church?

Lesson 26 - The Consummation
1 Thessalonians 1:8-10, 2 Thessalonians 2:1-4, Jude 20-23, Revelation 21:1-8

1. How does knowing the end of the Bible give us hope and confidence for today? What are some ways we can shift our focus from the temporary to the permanent?

2. In what ways does Satan tempt us to long for idols rather than God for fulfillment? What is the connection from turning from idols and waiting for Jesus to return?

3. What are some ways in which people in our culture actively oppose God? What are some common things we would expect people to do that follow the ways of the world?

4. What are some ways we can stay on guard against false teachings? What are some areas do you think Christians have the most trouble dealing within our culture?

5. Do you long to be in God's presence in your daily life? Why or why not? What are some things you would change to ensure time with Jesus?

Further Study

1. Can you recall a time when a life or death event took place and immediately rearranged your priorities?

2. How would you live your life differently if you knew Jesus was coming back this week? What would you pursue more? What would you set aside?

3. How does the knowledge of the wrath of God change the way you look at earthly desires? How does the truth that God will be the One to execute justice change the way you view those who have wronged you?

4. Do you sense a burden for those who don't know Christ? What are some ways you can live out and share the gospel in your daily life?

5. How do you view Heaven? Where does this basis come from? What areas in your life that have been broken by sin do you see being restored in Heaven?

Charts & Tables

The Ten Egyptian Plagues testify of Jesus Christ and His power to save.

Moses and Aaron are sent as messengers of the Lord, to Pharaoh, to instruct him to let the children of Israel go "so that they may serve the Lord." It is further stipulated that they must be allowed to travel a three days journey so that they may offer their sacrifices as a means of worship.

Pharaoh responds simply, "Who *is* the Lord, that I should obey his voice to let Israel go? I know not the Lord, neither will I let Israel go." Soon however, Pharaoh will find out who this God is, and why he should obey His voice. He will understand His power over all the other Egyptian gods and goddesses.

These ten Egyptian plagues not only demonstrated the power of God to Moses, the children of Israel, the Egyptians, and Pharaoh, but they were of such magnitude that they would be remembered for all generations, throughout the entire world. They again testify, as does both the Old and New Testament alike that salvation, from beginning to end, is only accomplished through Jesus Christ, "the author and finisher of our faith." (Heb 12:2)

Corresponding Egyptian God and Goddess to the type of plague:

Type of plague that God pronounced upon Egypt:

Hapi- Egyptian God of the Nile

Egyptian Plague- Water Turned to Blood

The first plague that was given to the Egyptians from God was that of turning the water to blood. As Aaron, the spokesman for Moses, touched the "rod" of the Lord to the Nile River it immediately turned to blood, all the fish died, and the river stank. Partially able to duplicate this miracle, the magicians of Pharaoh also turn water into blood, leaving Pharaoh unimpressed with this great wonder from God.

Seven days the water throughout all the land of Egypt remained in this state, unsuitable for drinking, the perfect length of time to demonstrate that the Lord was superior to all the other Gods of Egypt.

Heket- Egyptian Goddess of Fertility, Water, Renewal

Egyptian Plague- Frogs coming from the Nile River

Still, Pharaoh refused to let the children of Israel go from the presence of Egypt.

The second plague that was extended upon Egypt, from the "rod" by Aaron, was that of frogs. The frogs came up from the river and were in their houses, in their food, in their clothing, in every place possible. From the greatest to the least, no one in Egypt escaped the plague of frogs. Pharaoh's magicians were able to bring more frogs in their attempt to imitate the power of God, but only Moses was able to make the frogs go away. This was another attack on a famous Egyptian Goddess, Heket.

Geb- Egyptian God of the Earth

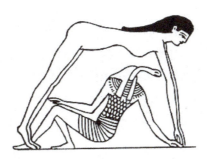

Egyptian Plague- Lice from the dust of the earth

Still Pharaoh would not concede, even after this display of power from the Lord, or magnificent plague, he would not let them go.

At the command of the Lord to Moses, Aaron was told to stretch forth his rod and smite the dust of the earth. When he did the dust became lice throughout all the land, on both people and beasts. The very dust that was referred to in the creation process of man is now used to plague men, as a reminder of his mortality and sin which both lead to death.

Finally, the magicians of Pharaoh are humiliated, being unable to compete with this power that was so much greater than themselves and the powers that they had from their Egyptian gods and goddesses, and they profess, "this is the finger of God." This was the last plague that required Aaron's involvement, as the next set of three plagues are issued by the word of Moses himself.

Khepri- Egyptian God of creation, movement of the Sun, rebirth

Egyptian Plague- Swarms of Flies

With the fourth Egyptian plague, which consisted of flies, begins the great miracle ot separation or differentiation. Moses met Pharaoh at the Nile River in the morning and made the demand, speaking on behalf of the Lord, "Let My peole go, that they may serve Me." Again, Pharaoh hardened his heart and disregarded the request, resulting in a pronouncement of swarms of flies.

This time, however, only the Egyptians are affected by the judgement, or plague, and the children of Israel remain unscathed. This wonder also moves the Egyptian plagues to a different level, adding destruction as well as discomfort to the consequence of their decisions.

Plagued by flies, Pharaoh tried a new tactic and begins bargaining with the Lord, showing his desire to maintain power and authority over God. He tries to dictate the terms and conditions of the offer, telling them they may sacrifice but only "in the land" clearly not complying with the requested "three days journey" that the Lord required. Moses wouldn't budge, and Pharaoh relented allowing them to leave, but telling them not to "go very far."

This temporary allowance is made solely to have Moses "intreat the Lord that the swarms of flies may depart", at this point Pharaoh has learned in part who the Lord is and asks for His assistance over the Egyptian gods and goddesses. As soon as the request is granted by the Lord, Pharaoh reneges on his promise and will not let them go, and continues to worship his Egyptian Gods.

Hathor-Egyptian Goddess of Love and Protection

Egyptian Plague- Death of Cattle and Livestock

Moses once again demanded of Pharaoh, "Let my people go, that they may serve me", revealing also the next Egytian plague to occur on the condition of continued disobedience to the request. This plague was given with an advanced warning, allowing a period of repentance to occur, which goes unheeded.

"Tomorrow" the hand of the Lord would be felt upon all the cattle and livestock, of only the Egyptians, as "grievous murrain." This means that disease and pestilence would fall upon their livestock with so severe a consequence as to cause them to die. This plague affected the Egyptian by creating a huge economic disaster, in areas of food, transportation, military supplies, farming, and economic goods that were produced by these livestock. Still Pharaohs heart remained hard and he would not listen to the Lord but remained faith to the Egytian gods and goddesses.

Isis- Egyptian Goddess of Medicine and Peace

Egyptian Plague- Ashes turned to Boils and Sores

Unannounced the sixth Egyptian plague is given, for the first time, directly attacking the Egyptian people themselves. Being instructed by the Lord, Moses took ashes from the furnace of affliction, and threw them into the air. As the dust from the ashes blew all over Egypt, it settled on man and beast alike in the form of boils and sores.

As with the previous two, throughout the remaining Egyptian plagues the division is drawn between the Egyptians and the children of Israel, as God gives protection to his covenant people. The severity of the judgment of God has now become personal, as it is actually felt by the people themselves.

Cleanliness being paramount in the Egyptian society, this plague pronounces the people "unclean." The magicians who have been seen throughout the previous plagues are unable to perform ceremonially rituals to their Egyptian Gods and Goddesses in this unclean state, not allowing them to even stand before Pharaoh; they are seen in the scriptural account no more. It is great to notice the contrast shown as Moses and Aaron are the only ones left standing in front of Pharaoh, with the "One True God" as their support.

Nut- Egyptian Goddess of the Sky

Egyptian Plague- Hail rained down in the form of fire

Again warning is given before the enactment of the plague takes place. Pharaoh is warned of the impending doom that will be faced if he does not listen to the Lord, and forget his own Egyptian gods and goddesses.

Hail of unspeakable size and ability to destroy, would rain down from the sky and turn to fire as it hit the ground. The Lord, in showing Pharaoh that "there is none like Him in the Earth", allows those who are willing to hear His word, and do as He commands, to be saved.

A division is now felt between the Egyptians in the form of those "converted" to the Lord, as shown by their obedience and willingness to escape to the protection of their "houses." Similarly we are warned to make our houses a place of refuge from the world today, we have been warned.

Interestingly enough, the crops that were destroyed by the hail consisted of flax and barley, which were ripening in the fields. These two particular crops were not the mainstay of their diet, but were used more specifically for their clothing and libations. This destruction would make their life uncomfortable, but as far as effecting their food supply , the wheat still survived. This gave the Egyptians still another chance to turn to "the One True God", and forsake their own Egyptian gods and goddesses, thus showing His mercy and grace even yet.

Seth- Egyptian God of Storms and Disorder

Egyptian Plague- Locusts sent from the sky

Still Pharaoh would not listen to the message of the Lord, still he relys on his own Egyptian gods and goddesses.

The eighth plague issued by the Lord had an even greater purpose than all the others, it was to be felt so that Pharaoh would tell even "his sons and son's sons" the mighty things of the Lord, thus teaching even future generations of the power of the "strong hand of God" over all the other Egyptian gods and goddesses.

Moses and Aaron approached Pharaoh with the same request, "Let my people go so that they may serve me", and pronounced the judgment of locusts if not heeded. This is the second wave of destruction to follow the hail, and whatever crops were left in tact after that display, were now completely consumed by the swarms of locusts that were unleashed from the sky. This wonder definitely affected their life source. By hitting them in their food supply, the Lord displayed the possibility of eminent death if a change of heart did not occur. Yet still, Pharaoh would not listen.

Ra- The Sun God

Egyptian Plague- Three Days of Complete Darkness

Darkness now fell upon Egypt, unannounced, as a prelude to the future fate to be felt by the Egyptian empire when the message of the Lord was not heeded, and they still turned to their own Egyptian gods and goddesses. Three days of palpable darkness, that was so immense it could be physically felt, covered the land of Egypt.

The sun, the most worshipped God in Egypt other than Pharaoh himself, gave no light. The Lord showed that he had control over the sun as a witness that the God of Israel had ultimate power over life and death. The psychological and religious impact would have had a profound influence on the Egyptians at this point. Darkness was a representation of death, judgment and hopelessness. Darkness was a complete absence of light.

Pharaoh- The Ultimate Power of Egypt

Egyptian Plague- Death of the Firstborn

Pharaoh, the king of Egypt, was worshipped by the Egyptians because he was considered to be the greatest Egyptian God of all. It was believed that he was actually the son of Ra himself, manifest in the flesh.

After the plague of darkness felt throughout the land was lifted, Pharaoh resumed his position of "bargaining with the Lord" and offered Moses another "deal." Since virtually all of the Egyptian animals had been consumed by the judgments of the Lord, Pharaoh now consented to the request made, to let the people go, but they must leave their animals behind.

This was a totally unacceptable offer, as the animals were to be used as the actual sacrifice to the Lord. The Lord is uncompromising when He has set the terms.

Enraged by the refusal, Pharaoh pronounced the last deadly plague to be unleashed upon the land from his very own lips as he warns Moses, "Get thee from me, take heed to thyself, see my face no more; for in *that* day thou seest my face thou shalt die."

And Moses said, "Thus saith the Lord, About midnight will I go out into the midst of Egypt: And all the firstborn in the land of Egypt shall die, from the firstborn of Pharaoh that sitteth upon his throne, even unto the firstborn of the maidservant that *is* behind the mill; and all the firstborn of beasts. And there shall be a great cry throughout all the land of Egypt, such as there was none like it, nor shall be like it any more." At this point the passive obedience that the children of Israel have shown is now moved to a level of active obedience. They are given strict instructions to follow so that they do not also feel the judgment of this last plague sent by the Lord. These instructions are known as "The Feast of Passover", "The Feast of Unleavened Bread", and "The Law of the Firstborn." In these rituals are displayed the law of sacrifice, the law of the gospel, and the law of consecration, all necessary requirements to receive ultimate salvation from spiritual death.

351 Old Testament Prophecies Fulfilled in Jesus Christ

Prophecy	Description	Fulfillment
1. Gen 3:15	Seed of a woman (virgin birth)	Gal 4:4-5; Matt 1:18
2. Gen 3:15	He will bruise Satan's head	Heb 2:14; 1 John 3:8
3. Gen 5:24	The bodily ascension to heaven illustrated	Mark 16:19
4. Gen 9:26-27	The God of Shem will be the Son of Shem	Luke 3:36
5. Gen 12:3	Seed of Abraham will bless all nations	Gal 3:8; Acts 3:25-26
6. Gen 12:7	The Promise made to Abraham's Seed	Gal 3:16
7. Gen 14:18	A priest after the order of Melchizedek	Heb 6:20
8. Gen 14:18	King of Peace and Righteousness	Heb 7:2
9. Gen 14:18	The Last Supper foreshadowed	Matt 26:26-29
10. Gen 17:19	Seed of Isaac (Gen 21:12)	Rom 9:7
11. Gen 22:8	The Lamb of God promised	John 1:29
12. Gen 22:18	As Isaac's seed, will bless all nations	Gal 3:16
13. Gen 26:2-5	The Seed of Isaac promised as the Redeemer	Heb 11:18
14. Gen 28:12	The Bridge to heaven	John 1:51
15. Gen 28:14	The Seed of Jacob	Luke 3:34
16. Gen 49:10	The time of His coming	Luke 2:1-7; Gal 4:4
17. Gen 49:10	The Seed of Judah	Luke 3:33
18. Gen 49:10	Called Shiloh or One Sent	John 17:3
19. Gen 49:10	Messiah to come before Judah lost identity	John 11:47-52
20. Gen 49:10	Unto Him shall the obedience of the people be	John 10:16
21. Ex 3:13-15	The Great "I AM"	John 4:26; 8:58
22. Ex 12:5	A Lamb without blemish	Heb 9:14; 1 Pet 1:19
23. Ex 12:13	The blood of the Lamb saves from wrath	Rom 5:8
24. Ex 12:21-27	Christ is our Passover	1 Cor 5:7
25. Ex 12:46	Not a bone of the Lamb to be broken	John 19:31-36
26. Ex 15:2	His exaltation predicted as Yeshua	Acts 7:55-56
27. Ex 15:11	His Character-Holiness	Luke 1:35; Acts 4:27
28. Ex 17:6	The Spiritual Rock of Israel	1 Cor 10:4
29. Ex 33:19	His Character-Merciful	Luke 1:72
30. Lev 1:2-9	His sacrifice a sweet smelling savor unto God	Eph 5:2
31. Lev 14:11	The leper cleansed-Sign to priesthood	Luke 5:12-14; Acts 6:7
32. Lev 16:15-17	Prefigures Christ's once-for-all death	Heb 9:7-14
33. Lev 16:27	Suffering outside the Camp	Matt 27:33; Heb. 13:11-12
34. Lev 17:11	The Blood-the life of the flesh	Matt 26:28; Mark 10:45
35. Lev 17:11	It is the blood that makes atonement	Rom. 3:23-24; 1 John 1:7
36. Lev 23:36-37	The Drink-offering: "If any man thirst"	John 7:37
37. Num 9:12	Not a bone of Him broken	John 19:31-36
38. Num 21:9	The serpent on a pole-Christ lifted up	John 3:14-18; 12:32
39. Num 24:17	Time: "I shall see him, but not now."	John 1:14; Gal 4:4
40. Deut 18:15	"This is of a truth that prophet"	John 6:14
41. Deut 18:15-16	"Had you believed Moses, you would believe me."	John 5:45-47
42. Deut 18:18	Sent by the Father to speak His word	John 8:28-29
43. Deut 18:19	Whoever will not hear must bear his sin	Acts 3:22-23
44. Deut 21:23	Cursed is he that hangs on a tree	Gal 3:10-13
45. Joshua 5:14-15	The Captain of our salvation	Heb 2:10
46. Ruth 4:4-10	Christ, our kinsman, has redeemed us	Eph 1:3-7
47. 1 Sam 2:35	A Faithful Priest	Heb. 2:17; 3:1-3, 6; 7:24-25
48. 1 Sam 2:10	Shall be an anointed King to the Lord	Matt 28:18; John 12:15

49. 2 Sam 7:12	David's Seed	Matt 1:1
50. 2 Sam 7:13	His Kingdom is everlasting	2 Pet 1:11
51. 2 Sam 7:14a	The Son of God	Luke 1:32; Rom 1:3-4
52. 2 Sam 7:16	David's house established forever	Luke 3:31; Rev 22:16
53. 2 Ki 2:11	The bodily ascension to heaven illustrated	Luke 24:51
54. 1 Chr 17:11	David's Seed	Matt 1:1; 9:27
55. 1 Chr 17:12-13	To reign on David's throne forever	Luke 1:32-33
56. 1 Chr 17:13	"I will be His Father, He...my Son."	Heb 1:5
57. Job 9:32-33	Mediator between man and God	1 Tim 2:5
58. Job 19:23-27	The Resurrection predicted	John 5:24-29
59. Psa 2:1-3	The enmity of kings foreordained	Acts 4:25-28
60. Psa 2:2	To own the title, Anointed (Christ)	John 1:41; Acts 2:36
61. Psa 2:6	His Character-Holiness	John 8:46; Rev 3:7
62. Psa 2:6	To own the title King	Matt 2:2
63. Psa 2:7	Declared the Beloved Son	Matt 3:17; Rom 1:4
64. Psa 2:7-8	The Crucifixion and Resurrection intimated	Acts 13:29-33
65. Psa 2:8-9	Rule the nations with a rod of iron	Rev 2:27; 12:5; 19:15
66. Psa 2:12	Life comes through faith in Him	John 20:31
67. Psa 8:2	The mouths of babes perfect His praise	Matt 21:16
68. Psa 8:5-6	His humiliation and exaltation	Heb 2:5-9
69. Psa 9:7-10	Judge the world in righteousness	Acts 17:31
70. Psa 16:10	Was not to see corruption	Acts 2:31; 13:35
71. Psa 16:9-11	Was to arise from the dead	John 20:9
72. Psa 17:15	The resurrection predicted	Luke 24:6
73. Psa 18:2-3	The horn of salvation	Luke 1:69-71
74. Psa 22:1	Forsaken because of sins of others	2 Cor 5:21
75. Psa 22:1	"My God, my God, why have You forsaken me?"	Matt 27:46
76. Psa 22:2	Darkness upon Calvary for three hours	Matt 27:45
77. Psa 22:7	They shoot out the lip and shake the head	Matt 27:39-44
78. Psa 22:8	"He trusted in God, let Him deliver Him"	Matt 27:43
79. Psa 22:9-10	Born the Savior	Luke 2:7
80. Psa 22:12-13	They seek His death	John 19:6
81. Psa 22:14	His blood poured out when they pierced His side	John 19:34
82. Psa 22:14-15	Suffered agony on Calvary	Mark 15:34-37
83. Psa 22:15	He thirsted	John 19:28
84. Psa 22:16	They pierced His hands and His feet	John 19:34-37; 20:27
85. Psa 22:17-18	Stripped Him before the stares of men	Luke 23:34-35
86. Psa 22:18	They parted His garments	John 19:23-24
87. Psa 22:20-21	He committed Himself to God	Luke 23:46
88. Psa 22:20-21	Satanic power bruising the Redeemer's heel	Heb 2:14
89. Psa 22:22	His Resurrection declared	John 20:17
90. Psa 22:27-28	He shall be the governor of the nations	Col 1:16
91. Psa 22:31	"It is finished"	John 19:30; Heb 10:10-12, 14, 18
92. Psa 23:1	"I am the Good Shepherd"	John 10:11; 1 Pet 2:25
93. Psa 24:3	His exaltation predicted	Acts 1:11; Phil 2:9
94. Psa 30:3	His resurrection predicted	Acts 2:32
95. Psa 31:5	"Into Your hands I commit my spirit"	Luke 23:46
96. Psa 31:11	His acquaintances fled from Him	Mark 14:50
97. Psa 31:13	They took counsel to put Him to death	Matt 27:1; John 11:53
98. Psa 31:14-15	"He trusted in God, let Him deliver him"	Matt 27:43
99. Psa 34:20	Not a bone of Him broken	John 19:31-36
100. Psa 35:11	False witnesses rose up against Him	Matt 26:59
101. Psa 35:19	He was hated without a cause	John 15:25
102. Psa 38:11	His friends stood afar off	Luke 23:49
103. Psa 38:12	Enemies try to entangle Him by craft	Mark 14:1; Matt 22:15
104. Psa 38:12-13	Silent before His accusers	Matt 27:12-14
105. Psa 38:20	He went about doing good	Acts 10:38
106. Psa 40:2-5	The joy of His resurrection predicted	John 20:20

#	Reference	Description	Fulfillment
107.	Psa 40:6-8	His delight-the will of the Father	John 4:34; Heb 10:5-10
108.	Psa 40:9	He was to preach the Righteousness in Israel	Matt 4:17
109.	Psa 40:14	Confronted by adversaries in the Garden	John 18:4-6
110.	Psa 41:9	Betrayed by a familiar friend	John 13:18
111.	Psa 45:2	Words of Grace come from His lips	John 1:17; Luke 4:22
112.	Psa 45:6	To own the title, God or Elohim	Heb 1:8
113.	Psa 45:7	A special anointing by the Holy Spirit	Matt 3:16; Heb. 1:9
114.	Psa 45:7-8	Called the Christ (Messiah or Anointed)	Luke 2:11
115.	Psa 45:17	His name remembered forever	Eph 1:20-21; Heb. 1:8
116.	Psa 55:12-14	Betrayed by a friend, not an enemy	John 13:18
117.	Psa 55:15	Unrepentant death of the Betrayer	Matt 27:3-5; Acts 1:16-19
118.	Psa 68:18	To give gifts to men	Eph 4:7-16
119.	Psa 68:18	Ascended into Heaven	Luke 24:51
120.	Psa 69:4	Hated without a cause	John 15:25
121.	Psa 69:8	A stranger to own brethren	John 1:11; 7:5
122.	Psa 69:9	Zealous for the Lord's House	John 2:17
123.	Psa 69:14-20	Messiah's anguish of soul before crucifixion	Matt 26:36-45
124.	Psa 69:20	"My soul is exceeding sorrowful"	Matt 26:38
125.	Psa 69:21	Given vinegar in thirst	Matt 27:34
126.	Psa 69:26	The Savior given and smitten by God	John 17:4; 18:11
127.	Psa 72:10-11	Great persons were to visit Him	Matt 2:1-11
128.	Psa 72:16	The corn of wheat to fall into the Ground	John 12:24-25
129.	Psa 72:17	Belief on His name will produce offspring	John 1:12-13
130.	Psa 72:17	All nations shall be blessed by Him	Gal 3:8
131.	Psa 72:17	All nations shall call Him blessed	John 12:13; Rev 5:8-12
132.	Psa 78:1-2	He would teach in parables	Matt 13:34-35
133.	Psa 78:2b	To speak the Wisdom of God with authority	Matt 7:29
134.	Psa 80:17	The Man of God's right hand	Mark 14:61-62
135.	Psa 88	The Suffering and Reproach of Calvary	Matt 27:26-50
136.	Psa 88:8	They stood afar off and watched	Luke 23:49
137.	Psa 89:27	Firstborn	Col 1:15-18
138.	Psa 89:27	Emmanuel to be higher than earthly kings	Luke 1:32-33
139.	Psa 89:35-37	David's Seed, throne, kingdom endure forever	Luke 1:32-33
140.	Psa 89:36-37	His character-Faithfulness	Rev 1:5; 19:11
141.	Psa 90:2	He is from everlasting (Micah 5:2)	John 1:1
142.	Psa 91:11-12	Identified as Messianic, used to tempt Christ	Luke 4:10-11
143.	Psa 97:9	His exaltation predicted	Acts 1:11; Eph 1:20
144.	Psa 100:5	His character-Goodness	Matt 19:16-17
145.	Psa 102:1-11	The Suffering and Reproach of Calvary	John 19:16-30
146.	Psa 102:25-27	Messiah is the Preexistent Son	Heb 1:10-12
147.	Psa 109:25	Ridiculed	Matt 27:39
148.	Psa 110:1	Son of David	Matt 22:42-43
149.	Psa 110:1	To ascend to the right-hand of the Father	Mark 16:19
150.	Psa 110:1	David's son called Lord	Matt 22:44-45
151.	Psa 110:4	A priest after Melchizedek's order	Heb 6:20
152.	Psa 112:4	His character-Compassionate, Gracious, et al	Matt 9:36
153.	Psa 118:17-18	Messiah's Resurrection assured	Luke 24:5-7; 1 Cor 15:20
154.	Psa 118:22-23	The rejected stone is Head of the corner	Matt 21:42-43
155.	Psa 118:26a	The Blessed One presented to Israel	Matt 21:9
156.	Psa 118:26b	To come while Temple standing	Matt 21:12-15
157.	Psa 132:11	The Seed of David (the fruit of His Body)	Luke 1:32; Act 2:30
158.	Psa 129:3	He was scourged	Matt 27:26
159.	Psa 138:1-6	The supremacy of David's Seed amazes kings	Matt 2:2-6
160.	Psa 147:3-6	The earthly ministry of Christ described	Luke 4:18
161.	Prov 1:23	He will send the Spirit of God	John 16:7
162.	Prov 8:23	Foreordained from everlasting	Rev 13:8; 1 Pet 1:19-20
163.	Song 5:16	The altogether lovely One	John 1:17
164.	Isa 2:3	He shall teach all nations	John 4:25

165. Isa 2:4	He shall judge among the nations	John 5:22
166. Isa 6:1	When Isaiah saw His glory	John 12:40-41
167. Isa 6:8	The One Sent by God	John 12:38-45
168. Isa 6:9-10	Parables fall on deaf ears	Matt 13:13-15
169. Isa 6:9-12	Blinded to Christ and deaf to His words	Acts 28:23-29
170. Isa 7:14	To be born of a virgin	Luke 1:35
171. Isa 7:14	To be Emmanuel-God with us	Matt 1:18-23; 1 Tim 3:16
172. Isa 8:8	Called Emmanuel	Matt 28:20
173. Isa 8:14	A stone of stumbling, a Rock of offense	1 Pet 2:8
174. Isa 9:1-2	His ministry to begin in Galilee	Matt 4:12-17
175. Isa 9:6	A child born-Humanity	Luke 1:31
176. Isa 9:6	A Son given-Deity	Luke 1:32; John 1:14; 1 Tim 3:16
177. Isa 9:6	Declared to be the Son of God with power	Rom 1:3-4
178. Isa 9:6	The Wonderful One, Peleh	Luke 4:22
179. Isa 9:6	The Counselor, Yaatz	Matt 13:54
180. Isa 9:6	The Mighty God, El Gibor	1 Cor 1:24; Titus 2:3
181. Isa 9:6	The Everlasting Father, Avi Adth	John 8:58; 10:30
182. Isa 9:6	The Prince of Peace, Sar Shalom	John 16:33
183. Isa 9:7	To establish an everlasting kingdom	Luke 1:32-33
184. Isa 9:7	His Character-Just	John 5:30
185. Isa 9:7	No end to his Government, Throne, and Peace	Luke 1:32-33
186. Isa 11:1	Called a Nazarene-the Branch, Netzer	Matt 2:23
187. Isa 11:1	A rod out of Jesse-Son of Jesse	Luke 3:23-32
188. Isa 11:2	Anointed One by the Spirit	Matt 3:16-17; Acts 10:38
189. Isa 11:2	His Character-Wisdom, Knowledge, et al	Col 2:3
190. Isa 11:3	He would know their thoughts	Luke 6:8; John 2:25
191. Isa 11:4	Judge in righteousness	Acts 17:31
192. Isa 11:4	Judges with the sword of His mouth	Rev 2:16; 19:11, 15
193. Isa 11:5	Character: Righteous & Faithful	Rev 19:11
194. Isa 11:10	The Gentiles seek Him	John 12:18-21
195. Isa 12:2	Called Jesus-Yeshua	Matt 1:21
196. Isa 22:22	The One given all authority to govern	Rev 3:7
197. Isa 25:8	The Resurrection predicted	1 Cor 15:54
198. Isa 26:19	His power of Resurrection predicted	Matt 27:50-54
199. Isa 28:16	The Messiah is the precious corner stone	Acts 4:11-12
200. Isa 28:16	The Sure Foundation	1 Cor 3:11; Matt 16:18
201. Isa 29:13	He indicated hypocritical obedience to His Word	Matt 15:7-9
202. Isa 29:14	The wise are confounded by the Word	1 Cor 1:18-31
203. Isa 32:2	A Refuge-A man shall be a hiding place	Matt 23:37
204. Isa 35:4	He will come and save you	Matt 1:21
205. Isa 35:5-6	To have a ministry of miracles	Matt 11:2-6
206. Isa 40:3-4	Preceded by forerunner	John 1:23
207. Isa 40:9	"Behold your God"	John 1:36; 19:14
208. Isa 40:10	He will come to reward	Rev 22:12
209. Isa 40:11	A shepherd-compassionate life-giver	John 10:10-18
210. Isa 42:1-4	The Servant-as a faithful, patient redeemer	Matt 12:18-21
211. Isa 42:2	Meek and lowly	Matt 11:28-30
212. Isa 42:3	He brings hope for the hopeless	John 4
213. Isa 42:4	The nations shall wait on His teachings	John 12:20-26
214. Isa 42:6	The Light (salvation) of the Gentiles	Luke 2:32
215. Isa 42:1-6	His is a worldwide compassion	Matt 28:19-20
216. Isa 42:7	Blind eyes opened	John 9:25-38
217. Isa 43:11	He is the only Savior	Acts 4:12
218. Isa 44:3	He will send the Spirit of God	John 16:7-13
219. Isa 45:21-25	He is Lord and Savior	Phil 3:20; Titus 2:13
220. Isa 45:23	He will be the Judge	John 5:22; Rom 14:11
221. Isa 46:9-10	Declares things not yet done	John 13:19
222. Isa 48:12	The First and the Last	John 1:30; Rev 1:8, 17

#	Reference	Description	Fulfillment
223.	Isa 48:16-17	He came as a Teacher	John 3:2
224.	Isa 49:1	Called from the womb-His humanity	Matt 1:18
225.	Isa 49:1	A Servant from the womb	Luke 1:31; Phil 2:7
226.	Isa 49:5	He will restore Israel	Acts 3:19-21; 15:16-17
227.	Isa 49:6	He is Salvation for Israel	Luke 2:29-32
228.	Isa 49:6	He is the Light of the Gentiles	John 8:12; Acts 13:47
229.	Isa 49:6	He is Salvation unto the ends of the earth	Acts 15:7-18
230.	Isa 49:7	He is despised of the Nation	John 1:11; 8:48-49; 19:14-15
231.	Isa 50:3	Heaven is clothed in black at His humiliation	Luke 23:44-45
232.	Isa 50:4	He is a learned counselor for the weary	Matt 7:29; 11:28-29
233.	Isa 50:5	The Servant bound willingly to obedience	Matt 26:39
234.	Isa 50:6a	"I gave my back to those who struck Me"	Matt 27:26
235.	Isa 50:6b	He was smitten on the cheeks	Matt 26:67
236.	Isa 50:6c	He was spat upon	Matt 27:30
237.	Isa 52:7	Published good tidings upon mountains	Matt 5:12; 15:29; 28:16
238.	Isa 52:13	The Servant exalted	Acts 1:8-11; Eph 1:19-22; Phil 2:5-9
239.	Isa 52:14	The Servant shockingly abused	Luke 18:31-34; Matt 26:67-68
240.	Isa 52:15	Nations startled by message of the Servant	Luke 18:31-34; Matt 26:67-68
241.	Isa 52:15	His blood shed sprinkles nations	Heb 9:13-14; Rev 1:5
242.	Isa 53:1	His people would not believe Him	John 12:37-38
243.	Isa 53:2	Appearance of an ordinary man	Phil 2:6-8
244.	Isa 53:3a	Despised	Luke 4:28-29
245.	Isa 53:3b	Rejected	Matt 27:21-23
246.	Isa 53:3c	Great sorrow and grief	Matt 26:37-38; Luke 19:41; Heb 4:15
247.	Isa 53:3d	Men hide from being associated with Him	Mark 14:50-52
248.	Isa 53:4a	He would have a healing ministry	Matt 8:16-17
249.	Isa 53:4b	Thought to be cursed by God	Matt 26:66; 27:41-43
250.	Isa 53:5a	Bears penalty for mankind's iniquities	2 Cor 5:21; Heb 2:9
251.	Isa 53:5b	His sacrifice provides peace between man and God	Col 1:20
252.	Isa 53:5c	His sacrifice would heal man of sin	1 Pet 2:24
253.	Isa 53:6a	He would be the sin-bearer for all mankind	1 John 2:2; 4:10
254.	Isa 53:6b	God's will that He bear sin for all mankind	Gal 1:4
255.	Isa 53:7a	Oppressed and afflicted	Matt 27:27-31
256.	Isa 53:7b	Silent before his accusers	Matt 27:12-14
257.	Isa 53:7c	Sacrificial lamb	John 1:29; 1 Pet 1:18-19
258.	Isa 53:8a	Confined and persecuted	Matt 26:47-27:31
259.	Isa 53:8b	He would be judged	John 18:13-22
260.	Isa 53:8c	Killed	Matt 27:35
261.	Isa 53:8d	Dies for the sins of the world	1 John 2:2
262.	Isa 53:9a	Buried in a rich man's grave	Matt 27:57
263.	Isa 53:9b	Innocent and had done no violence	Luke 23:41; John 18:38
264.	Isa 53:9c	No deceit in his mouth	1 Pet 2:22
265.	Isa 53:10a	God's will that He die for mankind	John 18:11
266.	Isa 53:10b	An offering for sin	Matt 20:28; Gal 3:13
267.	Isa 53:10c	Resurrected and live forever	Rom 6:9
268.	Isa 53:10d	He would prosper	John 17:1-5
269.	Isa 53:11a	God fully satisfied with His suffering	John 12:27
270.	Isa 53:11b	God's servant would justify man	Rom 5:8-9, 18-19
271.	Isa 53:11c	The sin-bearer for all mankind	Heb 9:28
272.	Isa 53:12a	Exalted by God because of his sacrifice	Matt 28:18
273.	Isa 53:12b	He would give up his life to save mankind	Luke 23:46
274.	Isa 53:12c	Numbered with the transgressors	Mark 15:27-28
275.	Isa 53:12d	Sin-bearer for all mankind	1 Pet 2:24
276.	Isa 53:12e	Intercede to God in behalf of mankind	Luke 23:34; Rom 8:34
277.	Isa 55:3	Resurrected by God	Acts 13:34
278.	Isa 55:4a	A witness	John 18:37

279. Isa 55:4b	He is a leader and commander	Heb 2:10
280. Isa 55:5	God would glorify Him	Acts 3:13
281. Isa 59:16a	Intercessor between man and God	Matt 10:32
282. Isa 59:16b	He would come to provide salvation	John 6:40
283. Isa 59:20	He would come to Zion as their Redeemer	Luke 2:38
284. Isa 60:1-3	He would show light to the Gentiles	Acts 26:23
285. Isa 61:1a	The Spirit of God upon him	Matt 3:16-17
286. Isa 61:1b	The Messiah would preach the good news	Luke 4:16-21
287. Isa 61:1c	Provide freedom from the bondage of sin	John 8:31-36
288. Isa 61:1-2a	Proclaim a period of grace	Gal 4:4-5
289. Jer 23:5-6	Descendant of David	Luke 3:23-31
290. Jer 23:5-6	The Messiah would be both God and Man	John 13:13; 1 Tim 3:16
291. Jer 31:22	Born of a virgin	Matt 1:18-20
292. Jer 31:31	The Messiah would be the new covenant	Matt 26:28
293. Jer 33:14-15	Descendant of David	Luke 3:23-31
294. Ezek 34:23-24	Descendant of David	Matt 1:1
295. Ezek 37:24-25	Descendant of David	Luke 1:31-33
296. Dan 2:44-45	The Stone that shall break the kingdoms	Matt 21:44
297. Dan 7:13-14a	He would ascend into heaven	Acts 1:9-11
298. Dan 7:13-14b	Highly exalted	Eph 1:20-22
299. Dan 7:13-14c	His dominion would be everlasting	Luke 1:31-33
300. Dan 9:24a	To make an end to sins	Gal 1:3-5
301. Dan 9:24a	To make reconciliation for iniquity	Rom 5:10; 2 Cor 5:18-21
302. Dan 9:24b	He would be holy	Luke 1:35
303. Dan 9:25	His announcement	John 12:12-13
304. Dan 9:26a	Cut off	Matt 16:21; 21:38-39
305. Dan 9:26b	Die for the sins of the world	Heb 2:9
306. Dan 9:26c	Killed before the destruction of the temple	Matt 27:50-51
307. Dan 10:5-6	Messiah in a glorified state	Rev 1:13-16
308. Hos 11:1	He would be called out of Egypt	Matt 2:15
309. Hos 13:14	He would defeat death	1 Cor 15:55-57
310. Joel 2:32	Offer salvation to all mankind	Rom 10:9-13
311. Jonah 1:17	Death and resurrection of Christ	Matt 12:40; 16:4
312. Mic 5:2a	Born in Bethlehem	Matt 2:1-6
313. Mic 5:2b	Ruler in Israel	Luke 1:33
314. Mic 5:2c	From everlasting	John 8:58
315. Hag 2:6-9	He would visit the second Temple	Luke 2:27-32
316. Hag 2:23	Descendant of Zerubbabel	Luke 2:27-32
317. Zech 3:8	God's servant	John 17:4
318. Zech 6:12-13	Priest and King	Heb 8:1
319. Zech 9:9a	Greeted with rejoicing in Jerusalem	Matt 21:8-10
320. Zech 9:9b	Beheld as King	John 12:12-13
321. Zech 9:9c	The Messiah would be just	John 5:30
322. Zech 9:9d	The Messiah would bring salvation	Luke 19:10
323. Zech 9:9e	The Messiah would be humble	Matt 11:29
324. Zech 9:9f	Presented to Jerusalem riding on a donkey	Matt 21:6-9
325. Zech 10:4	The cornerstone	Eph 2:20
326. Zech 11:4-6a	At His coming, Israel to have unfit leaders	Matt 23:1-4
327. Zech 11:4-6b	Rejection causes God to remove His protection	Luke 19:41-44
328. Zech 11:4-6c	Rejected in favor of another king	John 19:13-15
329. Zech 11:7	Ministry to "poor," the believing remnant	Matt 9:35-36
330. Zech 11:8a	Unbelief forces Messiah to reject them	Matt 23:33
331. Zech 11:8b	Despised	Matt 27:20
332. Zech 11:9	Stops ministering to those who rejected Him	Matt 13:10-11
333. Zech 11:10-11a	Rejection causes God to remove protection	Luke 19:41-44
334. Zech 11:10-11b	The Messiah would be God	John 14:7
335. Zech 11:12-13a	Betrayed for thirty pieces of silver	Matt 26:14-15
336. Zech 11:12-13b	Rejected	Matt 26:14-15

337. Zech 11:12-13c	Thirty pieces of silver cast in the house of the Lord	Matt 27:3-5	
338. Zech 11:12-13d	The Messiah would be God	John 12:45	
339. Zech 12:10a	The Messiah's body would be pierced	John 19:34-37	
340. Zech 12:10b	The Messiah would be both God and man	John 10:30	
341. Zech 12:10c	The Messiah would be rejected	John 1:11	
342. Zech 13:7a	God's will He die for mankind	John 18:11	
343. Zech 13:7b	A violent death	Mark 14:27	
344. Zech 13:7c	Both God and man	John 14:9	
345. Zech 13:7d	Israel scattered as a result of rejecting Him	Matt 26:31-56	
346. Zech 14:4	He would return to the Mt. of Olives	Acts 1:11-12	
347. Mal 3:1a	Messenger to prepare the way for Messiah	Mark 1:1-8	
348. Mal 3:1b	Sudden appearance at the temple	Mark 11:15-16	
349. Mal 3:1c	Messenger of the new covenant	Luke 4:43	
350. Mal 4:5	Forerunner in spirit of Elijah	Matt 3:1-3; 11:10-14; 17:11-13	
351. Mal 4:6	Forerunner would turn many to righteousness	Luke 1:16-17	

Sat 23 May 2015 / 5 Sivan 5775 B"H
Dr Maurice M. Mizrahi Congregation Adat Reyim Tikkun Lel Shavuot

The 613 Commandments

Introduction

Talmud: There are 613 commandments in the Torah:

-248 positive commandments (do's) and

-365 negative commandments (dont's).

> Rabbi Simlai, when preaching, said: 613 precepts were communicated to Moses: 365 negative precepts, corresponding to the number of solar days [in the year], and 248 positive precepts, corresponding to the number of members in a man's body [joints, or bones, covered with flesh and sinews, excluding teeth].
>
> Said Rabbi Hamnuna: What is the [proof] text for this? It is:
>
> *Torah tziva lanu Moshe; morasha kehillat Yaakov*
>
> Moses commanded us a Torah, an inheritance of the congregation of Jacob. [Deut. 33:4]
>
> In letter-value, Torah is 611. [Tav = 400, vav = 6, resh = 200, heh = 5, total 611.] [The first two of the Ten Commandments]:
>
> "I am [the Lord your God]" and "You shall have no [other Gods]"
>
> are [not counted here because] we heard [them directly] from the mouth of [God].
>
> [Makkot 23b-24a]

Known as "The Taryag", or "The 613". (613: tav = 400; resh = 200; yud = 10; gimel = 3.)

Strangely, Talmud provides no list.

Several rabbis have compiled lists. They generally agree on most, but disagree on whether some commandments are independent or part of other commandments. Example:

Rashi on Ner Tamid: God speaks to Moses about the mishkan, the Tabernacle, and says:

> And the fire upon the altar shall be burning... It shall not be put out... [Lev. 6:5]

And immediately, in the next verse, God clarifies:

> The fire upon the altar shall ALWAYS be burning. It shall not be put out. [Lev. 6:6] Rashi: Since "it shall not be put out" is stated twice in a row, if you extinguish the fire you transgress two negative commandments, not just one.

Rambam: No, the 2 are: One positive (P29, to keep the fire burning) and the other negative (N81, not to extinguish it).

Maimonides' *Sefer Hamitzvot (Ketab el Fara'id)* gives list most often used. He comments on each.

How many commandments apply today?

-Of the 613 commandments,

- only 411 don't require the Temple (202, or about a third, do);

- of these, only 369 commandments are applicable today (42 pertain to slaves, kings, nazirs, etc.);

- of these, only 270 apply always, regardless of circumstances (99 require special circumstances, e.g., "don't be late in fulfilling a vow" applies only if you make a vow; likewise, parapet around roof, paying laborer on time, etc.);

- of these, only 244 apply outside Israel. (26 apply only in Israel.) So, for most Jews, only 244, of 40%, of the mitzvot apply.

Can the commandments be summarized?

The mitzvot are not ranked by importance. Mishna:

> Rabbi [Yehudah haNasi] said: Be as scrupulous in observing a minor commandment as a major commandment, because you do not know the value of each commandment. [Pirkei Avot 2:1]

But Talmud tries to capture their essence:

[King] David came and reduced the [613 commandments] to eleven [principles], as it is written [in Psalm 15]:

> A Psalm of David.
>
> Lord, who shall abide in your tent? Who shall dwell in your holy mountain?
>
> (1) He who walks uprightly,
> (2) and does what is right,
> (3) and speaks the truth in his heart.
> (4) He who does not slander with his tongue,
> (5) nor does evil to his neighbor,
> (6) nor takes up a reproach against his neighbor.
> (7) In whose eyes a vile person is despised;
> (8) but he honors those who fear the Lord.
> (9) He who swears to his own hurt, and does not change.
> (10) He who does not put out his money at interest,
> (11) nor takes a bribe against the innocent.
>
> He who does these things shall never be moved... [Ps. 15]

[The prophet] Isaiah came and reduced them to six [principles], as it is written:

> (1) He who walks righteously,
> (2) and speaks uprightly;
> (3) he who despises the gain of oppression,
> (4) he who shakes his hands from holding bribes,
> (5) he who stops his ears from hearing of blood,
> (6) and shuts his eyes from seeing evil; He shall dwell on high... [Isa. 33:15-16]

[The prophet] Micah came and reduced them to three [principles], as it is written: It has been told you, O man, what is good, and what the Lord requires of you:

> (1) only to do justice,
> (2) and to love mercy,
> (3) and to walk humbly with your God... [Micah 6:8]

Again came [the prophet] Isaiah and reduced them to two [principles], as it is said:

> Thus says the Lord,
>
> (1) Keep justice,
> (2) and do righteousness... [Isa. 56:1]

[The prophet] Amos came and reduced them to one [principle], as it is said: For thus says the Lord to the house of Israel,

> (1) Seek me, and you shall live... [Amos 5:4]

But it is [the prophet] Habakuk who came and based them all on one [principle], as it is said:

> (1) But the righteous shall live by his faith. [Hab. 2:4] [Makkot 23b-24a]

The Ten Commandments' location in Torah

Why were the Ten Commandments not said at the beginning of the Torah? The Rabbis gave a parable. To what may this be compared? To the following: A king who entered a province said to the people, "May I be your king?" But the people said to him, "Have you done anything good to us that you should rule over us?" What did he do then? He built the city wall for them, he brought in the water supply for them, and he fought their battles. Then when he said to them, "May I be your king?", they said, "Yes".

Likewise, God. He brought the Israelites out of Egypt, divided the sea for them, sent down the manna for them, brought up the well for them, brought the quails for them, fought for them the battle with Amalek. Then He said to them, "I am to be your king". And they said to him, "Yes, yes".

[Mechilta de-Rabbi Ishmael, Exodus 20:2]

Rambam's 14 principles for inclusion:

1. Exclude the seven rabbinic commandments. (Wash hands for bread, build Eruv, say blessing before food, light Shabbat candles, read Megillah on Purim, light Hanukkah candles, recite Hallel.)

2. Exclude commandments derived with Rabbi Yishmael's 13 hermeneutic rules. (E.g., reverence for Torah scholars.)

3. Exclude commandments that are not permanent. (E.g., put blood on your houses so the Angel of Death passes over them.)

4. Exclude commandments that encompass the entire Torah. (E.g., "keep everything that I have instructed you".)

5. Do not consider the reason for a commandment as a separate commandment. (E.g., do not do this and do not bring guilt upon the land.)

6. Count a commandment with both positive and negative components as two. (E.g., on Shabbat, rest and do no work.)

7. Exclude the details of a commandment. (E.g., bring a sin-offering if can afford it; if not bring two birds; and if not bring a flour-offering.)

8. The negation of an obligation is not a prohibition.

9. An instruction repeated many times counts only once. (E.g., do not eat blood is repeated

7 times, but counts as only one commandment.)

10. Exclude preparations for a commandment.

11. Do not count the parts of a commandment separately. (E.g., the four species on Sukkot.)

12. Do not count separately the activities required to fulfill a commandment.

13. Count only once a commandment performed over many days.

14. Count each form of punishment only once, regardless of context.

Read Rambam's list of 613 mitzvot (below)

Cover some mitzvot in depth

Shavuot:

P45: The Shavuot Additional Offering P46: Bring Two Loaves on Shavuot P52: The three annual pilgrimages P54: Rejoicing on the Festivals.

> How does one rejoice? Sages: Go through the motions required by the holiday; get something special for yourself alone; do things differently; surround yourself with family, friends and community; consider it your duty to make sure THEY rejoice; and focus on only ONE source for rejoicing at a time.

P162: Resting on Shavuot

N156: Not to appear in Sanctuary on festival without sacrifice

P1: Believing in God. P3: Loving God.

P4: Fearing God.

> Rambam: Both fear and awe. How can these be commanded? Rambam was big on belief (13 principles), a point disputed by others.

> But Rambam: If you study God's work, you cannot but feel belief, love, and fear/awe. So are these just commandment to study? See also [Ber. 54a].

N363: A king not owning many horses N364: A king not taking many wives

N365: A king not amassing great personal wealth

Rambam: Use King Solomon as example. He thought that knowing (guessing) the reasons for commandments allowed him to satisfy the reasons while breaking the commandments. But God withheld reasons for commandments precisely so people would not do that to get around them.

N45: Not making cuttings in our flesh.

Tattoos not allowed. [Tosafot to Gittin 20b]

N64: Not testing God's promises and warnings.

Do not incur danger expecting a miracle.

N66: Not leaving the body of an executed criminal hanging overnight.

Kal vachomer (a fortiori): This applies to all dead.

N232: Failing to give charity to our needy brethren.

French Jews made their coffins from the boards of the tables on which they gave food to poor.

N235: Not lending at interest.

Modern poskim refuse to allow for inflation.

N250: Not wronging one another in business.

One-sixth rule: If amount in dispute less than 1/6 of total, no recourse.

N288: Not convicting on the testimony of a single witness

It once happened that Tobiah sinned and Zigud alone came and testified against him before Rav Papa. [But Rav Papa] punished Zigud [alone]!

[Zigud] exclaimed, "*He* sinned and *I* get punished!" "Yes", said [Rav Papa] to him, for it is written [in the Torah]:

> A single witness shall not rise up against a man [for any iniquity, or for any sin, in any sin that he sins; by the mouth of two witnesses, or by the mouth of three witnesses, shall the matter be established. [Deut. 19:15].

You have testified against him alone. All you did was bring him into disrepute.

[Pes. 113b]

N290: No capital punishment based on circumstantial evidence. N294: Not punishing a person for a sin committed under duress. N300: Not inflicting excessive corporal punishment.

> Rules: No permanent injury must result; one must first estimates how many strokes the defendant can bear, etc. Practice stopped in Middle Ages, replaced by fines.

N299: Not giving misleading advice.

> "Stumbling block before the blind" also applies to causing another to sin, or even goading someone into anger, which provoke him to sin.

N313: Not to add to the Written or Oral Law. N314: Not to detract from the Written or Oral Law

> Some latitude in interpretation allowed, on case by case basis

The 613 *Mitzvot*
(Commandments)
According to the Rambam

248 Positive Mitzvot

Mitzvot aseh

P1: Believing in God
P2: Unity of God
P3: Loving God
P4: Fearing God
P5: Worshiping God
P6: Cleaving to God
P7: Taking an oath by God's Name
P8: Walking in God's ways
P9: Sanctifying God's Name
P10: Reading the Shema twice daily
P11: Studying and teaching Torah
P12: Wearing Tephillin of the head
P13: Wearing Tephillin of the hand
P14: To make Tzitzit
P15: To affix a Mezuzah
P16: Hakhel during Sukkot
P17: A king should write a Torah
P18: Everyone should write a Torah
P19: Grace after meals
P20: Building a Sanctuary for God
P21: Revering the Beis Hamikdosh

P22: Guarding the Mikdosh
P23: Levitical services in the Mikdosh
P24: Ablutions of the Kohanim
P25: Kindling the lamps by the Kohanim
P26: Kohanim blessing Israel
P27: The Showbread
P28: Burning the Incense
P29: The perpetual fire on the Altar
P30: Removing the ashes from the Altar
P31: Removing tameh persons from the camp
P32: Honoring the Kohanim P33: The Priestly garments
P34: Kohanim bearing the Ark on their shoulders
P35: The oil of the Anointment
P36: Kohanim ministering in watches
P37: Kohanim defiling themselves for deceased relatives
P38: Kohen Gadol should only marry a virgin
P39: Daily Burnt Offerings P40: Kohen Gadol's daily Meal Offering
P41: The Shabbat Additional Offering
P42: The New Moon Additional Offering
P43: The Pesach Additional Offering
P44: The Meal Offering of the Omer
P45: The Shavuot Additional Offering
P46: Bring Two Loaves on Shavuot
P47: The Rosh Hashana Additional Offering
P48: The Yom Kippur Additional Offering
P49: The Service of Yom Kippur
P50: The Sukkot Offering
P51: The Shemini Atzeret Additional Offering
P52: The three annual pilgrimages
P53: Appearing before the Lord during the Festivals
P54: Rejoicing on the Festivals
P55: Slaughtering the Pesach Offering
P56: Eating the Pesach Offering
P57: Slaughtering the Pesach Sheni Offering
P58: Eating the Pesach Sheni Offering
P59: Blowing the trumpets in the Sanctuary
P60: Minimum age of cattle to be offered
P61: Offering only unblemished sacrifices
P62: Bringing salt with every offering
P63: The Burnt-Offering
P64: The Sin-Offering
P65: The Guilt-Offering
P66: The Peace-Offering
P67: The Meal-Offering
P68: Offerings of a Court that has erred
P69: The Fixed Sin-Offering
P70: The Suspensive Guilt-Offering
P71: The Unconditional Guilt-Offering
P72: The Offering of a Higher or Lower Value
P73: Making confession
P74: Offering brought by a zav (man with a discharge)
P75: Offering brought by a zavah (woman with a discharge)
P76: Offering of a woman after childbirth
P77: Offering brought by a leper
P78: Tithe of Cattle
P79: Sanctifying the Firstborn P80: Redeeming the First-born
P81: Redeeming the firstling of a donkey
P82: Breaking the neck of the firstling of a donkey
P83: Bringing due offerings on the first festival
P84: All offerings to be brought to the Sanctuary
P85: Bring all offerings due from outside Eretz Yisrael to Sanctuary
P86: Redeeming blemished offerings

P87: Holiness of substituted offerings
P88: Kohanim eat the residue of the Meal Offerings
P89: Kohanim eat the meat of the Consecrated Offerings
P90: To burn Consecrated Offerings that have become tameh
P91: To burn the remnant of the Consecrated Offerings
P92: The Nazir letting his hair grow
P93: Nazirite obligations on completion of vow
P94: All oral submissions to be fulfilled
P95: Revocation of vows
P96: Defilement through carcasses of animals
P97: Defilement through carcasses of eight creeping creatures
P98: Defilement of food and drink
P99: Tumah of a menstruant
P100: Tumah of a woman after childbirth
P101: Tumah of a leper
P102: Garments contaminated by leprosy
P103: A leprous house
P104: Tumah of a zav (man with a discharge)
P105: Tumah of semen
P106: Tumah of a zavah (woman with a discharge)
P107: Tumah of a corpse
P108: The law of the water of sprinkling
P109: Immersing in a mikveh
P110: Cleansing from Leprosy
P111: A leper must shave his head
P112: The leper must be made distinguishable
P113: Ashes of the Red Heifer
P114: Valuation of a person
P115: Valuation of beasts
P116: Valuation of houses
P117: Valuation of fields
P118: Restitution for Sacrilege
P119: The fruits of the fourth- year planting
P120: To leave the corners (Peah) for the poor
P121: To leave gleanings for the poor
P122: To leave the forgotten sheaf for the poor
P123: To leave defective grape clusters for the poor
P124: To leave grape gleanings for the poor
P125: To bring First-fruits to the Sanctuary
P126: To set aside the great Heaveoffering
P127: To set aside the first tithe
P128: To set aside the second tithe
P129: The Levites' tithe for the Kohanim
P130: To set aside the poor- man's tithe in the third and sixth year
P131: The avowal of the tithe
P132: Recital on bringing the First-fruits
P133: To set aside the Challah for the Kohen
P134: Renouncing as ownerless produce of the Sabbatical year
P135: Resting the land on the Sabbatical year
P136: Sanctifying the Jubilee year
P137: Blowing the Shofar in the Jubilee year
P138: Reversion of the land in the Jubilee year
P139: Redemption of property in a walled city
P140: Counting the years till the Jubilee year
P141: Canceling monetary claims in the Sabbatical year
P142: Exacting debts from idolaters
P143: The Kohen's due in the slaughter of every clean animal
P144: The first of the fleece to be given to the Kohen
P145: Devoted thing to God and the Kohen
P146: Slaughtering animals before eating them
P147: Covering the blood of slain birds and animals

P148: Releasing the mother before taking the nest
P149: Searching for the prescribed signs in cattle and animals
P150: Searching for the prescribed signs in birds
P151: Searching for the prescribed signs in grasshoppers
P152: Searching for the prescribed signs in fishes
P153: Determining the New Moon
P154: Resting on Shabbat P155: Proclaiming the sanctity of Shabbat
P156: Removal of chametz on Pesach
P157: Recounting Exodus from Egypt on first night of Pesach
P158: Eating Matzah on the first night of Pesach
P159: Resting on the first day of Pesach
P160: Resting on the seventh day of Pesach
P161: Counting the Omer P162: Resting on Shavuot
P163: Resting on Rosh Hashana
P164: Fasting on Yom Kippur
P165: Resting on Yom Kippur
P166: Resting on the first day of Sukkot
P167: Resting on Shemini Atzeret
P168: Dwelling in a Sukkah for seven days
P169: Taking a Lulav on Sukkot
P170: Hearing a Shofar on Rosh Hashana
P171: Giving half a shekel annually
P172: Heeding the Prophets
P173: Appointing a King
P174: Obeying the Great Court
P175: Abiding by a majority decision
P176: Appointing Judges and Officers of the Court
P177: Treating litigants equally before the law
P178: Testifying in Court
P179: Inquiring into the testimony of witnesses
P180: Condemning witnesses who testify falsely
P181: Eglah Arufah
P182: Establishing Six Cities of Refuge
P183: Assigning cities to the Levi'im
P184: Building fences on roof; and removing sources of danger from our dwellings
P185: Destroying all idol- worship
P186: The law of the apostate city
P187: The law of the Seven Nations
P188: The extinction of the seed of Amalek
P189: Remembering the nefarious deeds of Amalek
P190: The law of the non- obligatory war
P191: Appoint a Kohen to speak to the people going to war and send back any man unfit for battle
P192: Preparing a place beyond the camp
P193: Including a digging tool among war implements
P194: A robber to restore the stolen article
P195: To give charity
P196: Lavishing gifts on a Hebrew bondman on his freedom
P197: Lending money to the poor
P198: Lending money to the heathen with interest
P199: Restoring a pledge to a needy owner
P200: Paying wages on time
P201: An employee is allowed to eat the produce he's working in
P202: Unloading a tired animal
P203: Assisting the owner in loading his burden
P204: Returning lost property to its owner
P205: Rebuking the sinner
P206: Loving our Fellow Jew
P207: Loving the convert
P208: The law of weights and measures
P209: Honoring scholars
P210: Honoring parents

P211: Fearing parents
P212: Be fruitful and multiply
P213: The law of marriage
P214: Bridegroom devotes himself to his wife for one year
P215: Circumcising one's son
P216: Law of the Levirite Marriage
P217: Law of Chalitzah
P218: A violator must marry the maiden he has violated
P219: The law of the defamer of his bride
P220: The law of the seducer
P221: The law of the captive woman
P222: The law of divorce
P223: The law of a suspected adulteress
P224: Whipping transgressors of certain commandments
P225: The law of unintentional manslaughter
P226: Beheading transgressors of certain commandments
P227: Strangling transgressors of certain commandments
P228: Burning transgressors of certain commandments
P229: Stoning transgressors of certain commandments
P230: Hanging after execution, transgressors of certain commandments
P231: Burial on the day of execution
P232: The law of the Hebrew bondman
P233: Hebrew bondmaid to be married by her master or his son
P234: Redemption of a Hebrew bondmaid
P235: The law of a Canaanite bondman
P236: Penalty of inflicting injury
P237: The law of injuries caused by an ox
P238: The law of injuries caused by an pit
P239: The law of theft
P240: The law of damage caused by a beast
P241: The law of damage caused by a fire
P242: The law of an unpaid bailee
P243: The law of a paid bailee
P244: The law of a borrower
P245: The law of buying and selling
P246: The law of litigants
P247: Saving the life of the pursued
P248: The law of inheritance

365 Negative Mitzvot

Mitzvot lo taaseh

N1: Not believing in any other God
N2: Not to make images for the purpose of worship
N3: Not to make an idol (even for others) to worship
N4: Not to make figures of human beings
N5: Not to bow down to an idol
N6: Not to worship idols
N7: Not to hand over any children to Moloch
N8: Not to practice sorcery of the ov
N9: Not to practice sorcery of the yidde'oni
N10: Not to study idolatrous practices
N11: Not to erect a pillar which people will assemble to honor
N12: Not to make figured stones on which to prostrate ourselves
N13: Not to plant trees in the Sanctuary
N14: Not to swear by an idol
N15: Not to divert people to idolatry

N16: Not to try to persuade an Israelite to worship idols
N17: Not to love someone who seeks to mislead you to idols
N18: Not to relax one's aversion to the misleader
N19: Not to save the life of a misleader
N20: Not to plead for the misleader
N21: Not to oppress evidence unfavorable to the misleader
N22: No benefit from ornaments which have adorned an idol
N23: Not rebuilding an apostate city
N24: Not deriving benefit from property of an apostate city
N25: Not increasing wealth from anything connected with idolatry
N26: Not prophesying in the name of an idol
N27: Not prophesying falsely
N28: Not to listen to the prophesy made in the name of an idol
N29: Not fearing or refraining from killing a false prophet
N30: Not adopting the habits and customs of unbelievers
N31: Not practicing divination
N32: Not regulating one's conduct by the stars
N33: Not practicing the art of the soothsayer
N34: Not practicing sorcery
N35: Not practicing the art of the charmer
N36: Not consulting a necromancer who uses the ov
N37: Not consulting a sorcerer who uses the ydo'a
N38: Not to seek information from the dead
N39: Women not to wear men's clothes or adornments
N40: Men not wearing women's clothes or adornments
N41: Not imprinting any marks on our bodies
N42: Not wearing Shatnes (mixture of wool and linen)
N43: Not shaving the temples of the head
N44: Not shaving the beard
N45: Not making cuttings in our flesh
N46: Not settling in the land of Egypt
N47: Not to follow one's heart or eyes
N48: Not to make a covenant with the Seven Nations of Canaan
N49: Not to spare the life of the Seven Nations
N50: Not to show mercy to idolaters
N51: Not to allow idolaters to settle in our land
N52: Not to intermarry with a heretic
N53: Not to intermarry with a male from Ammon or Moav
N54: Not to exclude the descendants of Esav
N55: Not to exclude the descendants of Egyptians
N56: Not offering peace to Ammon and Moav
N57: Not destroying fruit trees in time of siege
N58: Not fearing heretics in time of war
N59: Not forgetting what Amalek did to us
N60: Not blaspheming the Great Name
N61: Not violating a shevuas bittui (oath of utterance)
N62: Not swearing a shevuas shav (vain oath)
N63: Not profaning the Name of God
N64: Not testing His promises and warnings
N65: Not to break down houses of worship or to destroy holy books
N66: Not leaving the body of an executed criminal hanging overnight
N67: Not to interrupt the watch over the Sanctuary
N68: Kohen Gadol may not enter Sanctuary at any but prescribed times
N69: Kohen with blemish not to enter Sanctuary from Altar inwards
N70: Kohen with a blemish not to minister in the Sanctuary
N71: Kohen with a temporary blemish not to minister in Sanctuary
N72: Levites and Kohanim not perform each other's allotted services
N73: Not to be intoxicated when entering Sanctuary; and not to be intoxicated when giving a decision on Torah law
N74: Zar (nonkohen) not to minister in Sanctuary
N75: Tameh Kohen not to minister in Sanctuary
N76: Kohen who is tevul yom, not to minister in Sanctuary
N77: Tameh person not to enter any part of Sanctuary

N78: Tameh person not to enter camp of Levites
N79: Not to build an Altar of stones which were touched by iron
N80: Not to ascend the Altar by steps
N81: Not to extinguish the Altar fire
N82: Not to offer any sacrifice whatever on the Golden Altar
N83: Not to make oil like the Oil of Anointment
N84: Not anoint anyone with special oil except Kohen Gadol and King
N85: Not to make incense like used in Sanctuary
N86: Not to remove the
staves from their rings in the Ark
N87: Not to remove the Breastplate from the Ephod
N88: Not to tear the edge of the Kohen Gadol's robe N89: Not to offer sacrifices outside the Sanctuary Court
N90: Not to slaughter holy offerings outside the Sanctuary Court
N91: Not to dedicate a blemished animal to be offered on the Altar
N92: Not to slaughter a blemished animal as a korban
N93: Not to dash the blood of a blemished beast on the Altar
N94: Not to burn the sacrificial portions of blemished beast on Altar
N95: Not to sacrifice a beast with a temporary blemish
N96: Not to offer a blemished sacrifice of a gentile
N97: Not to cause an offering to become blemished
N98: Not to offer leaven or honey upon the Altar
N99: Not to offer a sacrifice without salt
N100: Not to offer on Altar the "hire of a harlot" or "price of a dog"
N101: Not to slaughter the mother and her young on the same day
N102: Not to put olive oil on the Meal-Offering of a sinner
N103: Not to put frankincense the Meal- Offering of a sinner
N104: Not mingle olive oil with Meal-Offering of suspected adulteress
N105: Not put frankincense on Meal-Offering of suspected adulteress
N106: Not to change a beast that has been consecrated as an offering
N107: Not to change one's holy offering for another
N108: Not to redeem the firstling (of a clean beast)
N109: Not to sell the tithe of cattle
N110: Not to sell devoted property
N111: Not redeem devoted land without specific statement of purpose
N112: Not to sever the head of the bird of Sin-Offering during melikah
N113: Not to do any work with a dedicated beast
N114: Not to shear a dedicated beast
N115: Not slaughter the Korban Pesach while chametz in our possession
N116: Not leave any sacrificial portions of Korban Pesach overnight
N117: Not allow meat of Korban Pesach to remain till morning
N118: Not allow meat of 14 Nissan Festival Offering remain till day 3:
N119: Not allow meat of Pesach Sheni offering to remain till morning
N120: Not allow meat of thanksgiving offering to remain till morning
N121: Not to break any bones of Pesach offering
N122: Not to break any bones of Pesach Sheni offering
N123: Not to remove Pesach offering from where it is eaten
N124: Not to bake the residue of a meal offering with leaven
N125: Not to eat the Pesach offering boiled or raw
N126: Not to allow a ger toshav to eat the Pesach offering
N127: An uncircumcised person may not eat the Pesach offering
N128: Not to allow an apostate Israelite to eat the Pesach offering
N129: Tameh person may not eat hallowed food
N130: Not to eat meat of consecrated offerings which have become tameh
N131: Not eating nosar (beyond allotted time)
N132: Not eating piggul (improper intentions)
N133: A zar may not eat terumah
N134: A Kohen's tenant or hired servant may not eat terumah
N135: An uncircumcised Kohen may not eat terumah
N136: Tameh Kohen may not eat terumah
N137: A chalalah may not eat holy food
N138: Not to eat the Meal- Offering of a Kohen
N139: Not eat Sin-Offering meat whose blood was brought into Sanctuary

N140: Not to eat the invalidated consecrated offerings
N141: Not to eat unredeemed 2nd tithe of corn outside Yerushalayim
N142: Not consuming unredeemed 2nd tithe of wine outside Yerushalayim
N143: Not consuming unredeemed 2nd tithe of oil outside Yerushalayim
N144: Not eating an unblemished firstling outside Yerushalayim
N145: Not eat sin-offering and guilt-offering outside Sanctuary court
N146: Not to eat the meat of a burnt offering
N147: Not eat lesser holy offerings before blood dashed on Altar
N148: A zar not to eat the most holy offerings
N149: Kohen not to eat first fruits outside Yerushalayim
N150: Not eating an unredeemed tameh 2nd tithe, even in Yerushalayim
N151: Not eating the 2nd tithe in mourning
N152: Not spend 2nd tithe redemption money, except on food and drink
N153: Not eating tevel(produce heaveoffering and tithes not taken)
N154: Not altering the prescribed order of harvest tithing
N155: Not to delay payment of vows
N156: Not to appear in Sanctuary on festival without sacrifice
N157: Not to infringe on any oral obligation, even if without an oath
N158: Kohen may not marry a zonah
N159: Kohen may not marry a chalalah
N160: Kohen may not marry a divorcee
N161: Kohen Gadol may not marry a widow
N162: Kohen Gadol may not have relations with a widow
N163: Kohen with disheveled hair may not enter the Sanctuary
N164: Kohen wearing rent garments may not enter Sanctuary
N165: Ministering Kohanim may not leave the Sanctuary
N166: Common Kohen may not defile himself for dead (except some)
N167: Kohen Gadol may not be under one roof with dead body
N168: Kohen Gadol may not defile himself for any dead person
N169: Levites may not take a share of the land
N170: Levites may not share in the spoil on conquest of the Land
N171: Not to tear out hair for the dead
N172: Not to eat any unclean animal
N173: Not to eat any unclean fish
N174: Not to eat any unclean fowl
N175: Not to eat any swarming winged insect
N176: Not to eat anything which swarms on the earth
N177: Not to eat any creeping thing that breeds in decayed matter
N178: Not to eat living creatures that breed in seeds or fruit
N179: Not to eat any swarming thing
N180: Not to eat any animal which is a nevelah
N181: Not to eat an animal which is a treifah
N182: Not to eat a limb of a living animal
N183: Not to eat the gid hanasheh (sinew of the thigh- vein)
N184: Not to eat blood N185: Not to eat the fat of a clean animal
N186: Not to cook meat in milk
N187: Not to eat meat cooked in milk
N188: Not to eat the flesh of a stoned ox
N189: Not to eat bread made from grain of new crop
N190: Not to eat roasted grain of the new crop
N191: Not to eat fresh ears of grain
N192: Not to eat orlah N193: Not to eat kilai hakerem
N194: Not to drink yayin nesach (libation wine for idol worship)
N195: No eating or drinking to excess
N196: Not to eat on Yom Kippur
N197: Not to eat chametz on Pesach
N198: Not to eat an admixture of chametz on Pesach
N199: Not to eat chametz after noon of 14 Nissan
N200: No chametz may be seen in our homes during Pesach
N201: Not to possess chametz during Pesach
N202: A Nazir may not drink wine

N203: A Nazir may not eat fresh grapes
N204: A Nazir may not eat dried grapes
N205: A Nazir may not eat grape kernels
N206: A Nazir may not eat grape husks
N207: A Nazir may not rend himself tameh for the dead
N208: A Nazir may not rend himself tameh by entering house with corpse
N209: A Nazir may not shave N210: Not to reap all harvest without leaving a corner for the poor
N211: Not to gather ears of corn that fell during harvesting
N212: Not to gather the whole produce of vineyard at vintage time
N213: Not to gather single fallen grapes during the vintage
N214: Not to return for a forgotten sheaf
N215: Not to sow kilayim (diverse kinds of seed in one field)
N216: Not to sow grain or vegetables in a vineyard
N217: Not to make animals of different species
N218: Not to work with two different kinds of animals together
N219: Not preventing a beast from eating the produce where working
N220: Not to cultivate the soil in the seventh year
N221: Not to prune the trees in the seventh year
N222: Not reap a selfgrown plant in the 7th year as in ordinary year
N223: Not gather selfgrown fruit in the 7th year as in ordinary year
N224: Not to cultivate the soil in the Jubilee year
N225: Not to reap the aftergrowths of Jubilee year as in ordinary year

N226: Not to gather fruit in Jubilee year as in ordinary year
N227: Not to sell out holdings in Eretz Israel in perpetuity
N228: No to sell the open lands of the Levites
N229: Not to forsake the Levites
N230: Not to demand payment of debts after Shmitah year
N231: Not to withhold a loan to be canceled by the Shmitah year
N232: Failing to give charity to our needy brethren
N233: Not sending a Hebrew bondman away emptyhanded
N234: Not demanding payment from a debtor known unable to pay
N235: Not lending at interest N236: Not borrowing at interest
N237: Not participating in a loan at interest
N238: Not oppressing an employee by delaying payment of his wages
N239: Not taking a pledge from a debtor by force
N240: Not keeping a needed pledge from its owner
N241: Not taking a pledge from a widow
N242: Not taking food utensils in pledge
N243: Not abducting an Israelite
N244: Not stealing money
N245: Not committing robbery
N246: Not fraudulently altering land boundaries
N247: Not usurping our debts N248: Not repudiating our debts
N249: Not to swear falsely in repudiating our debts
N250: Not wronging one another in business
N251: Not wronging one another by speech
N252: Not wronging a proselyte by speech
N253: Not wronging a proselyte in business
N254: Not handing over a fugitive bondman
N255: Not wronging a fugitive bondman
N256: Not dealing harshly with orphans and widows
N257: Not employing a Hebrew bondman in degrading tasks
N258: Not selling a Hebrew bondman by public auction
N259: Not having a Hebrew bondman do unnecessary work
N260: Not allowing a heathen to mistreat a Hebrew bondman
N261: Not selling a Hebrew bondmaid
N262: Not to afflict one's wife or espoused Hebrew bondmaid by diminishing food, raiment or conjugal rights
N263: Not selling a captive woman
N264: Not enslaving a captive woman
N265: Not planning to acquire someone else's property
N266: Not coveting another's belongings
N267: A hired laborer not eating growing crops

N268: A hired laborer not putting of the harvest in his own vessel
N269: Not ignoring lost property
N270: Not leaving a person who is trapped under his burden
N271: Not cheating in measurements and weights
N272: Not keeping false weights and measures
N273: Judge not to commit unrighteousness
N274: Judge not accept gifts from litigants
N275: Judge not to favor a litigant
N276: Judge not avoid just judgment through fear of a wicked person
N277: Judge not to decide in favor of poor man, out of pity
N278: Judge not to pervert justice against person of evil repute
N279: Judge not to pity one who has killed or caused loss of limb
N280: Judge not perverting justice due to proselytes or orphans
N281: Judge not to listen to one litigant in absence of the other
N282: A court may not convict by a majority of one in a capital case
N283: A judge may not rely on the opinion of a fellow judge, or may not argue for conviction after favoring acquittal
N284: Not appointing an unlearned judge
N285: Not bearing false witness
N286: Judge not to receive a wicked man's testimony
N287: Judge not to receive testimony from litigant's relatives
N288: Not convicting on the testimony of a single witness
N289: Not killing a human being
N290: No capital punishment based on circumstantial evidence
N291: A witness not acting as an advocate
N292: Not killing a murderer without trial
N293: Not sparing the life of a pursuer
N294: Not punishing a person for a sin committed under duress
N295: Not accepting ransom from an unwitting murderer
N296: Not accepting a ransom from a wilful murderer
N297: Not neglecting to save the life of an Israelite in danger
N298: Not leaving obstacles on public or private domain
N299: Not giving misleading advice
N300: Not inflicting excessive corporal punishment
N301: Not to bear tales
N302: Not to hate another Jew
N303: Not to put another to shame
N304: Not to take vengeance on another
N305: Not to bear a grudge
N306: Not to take the entire bird's nest (mother and young)
N307: Not to shave the scall
N308: Not to cut or cauterize signs of leprosy
N309: Not ploughing a valley where Eglah Arufah was done
N310: Not permitting a sorcerer to live
N311: Not taking bridegroom from home during first year
N312: Not to differ from traditional authorities
N313: Not to add to the Written or Oral Law
N314: Not to detract from the Written or Oral Law
N315: Not to curse a judge
N316: Not to curse a ruler
N317: Not to curse any Israelite
N318: Not cursing parents
N319: Not smiting parents
N320: Not to work on Shabbat
N321: Not to go beyond city limits on Shabbat
N322: Not to punish on Shabbat
N323: Not to work on the first day of Pesach
N324: Not to work on the seventh day of Pesach
N325: Not to work on Atzeret
N326: Not to work on Rosh Hashana
N327: Not to work on the first day of Sukkot
N328: Not to work on Shemini Atzeret

N329: Not to work on Yom Kippur
N330: Not have relations with one's mother
N331: Not have relations with one's father's wife
N332: Not have relations with one's sister
N333: Not have relations with daughter of father's wife if sister
N334: Not have relations with one's son's daughter
N335: Not have relations with one's daughter's daughter N336: Not have relations with one's daughter
N337: Not have relations with a woman and her daughter N338: Not have relations with a woman and her son's daughter
N339: Not have relations with a woman and her daughter's daughter
N340: Not have relations with one's father's sister
N341: Not have relations with one's mother's sister
N342: Not have relations with wife of father's brother
N343: Not have relations with one's son's wife
N344: Not have relations with brother's wife
N345: Not have relations with sister of wife (during her lifetime)
N346: Not to have relations with a menstruant
N347: Not to have relations with another man's wife
N348: Men may not lie with beasts
N349: Women may not lie with beasts
N350: A man may not lie carnally with another man
N351: A man may not lie carnally with his father
N352: A man may not lie carnally with his father's brother
N353: Not to be intimate with a kinswoman
N354: A mamzer may not have relations with a Jewess
N355: Not having relations with a woman without marriage
N356: Not remarrying one's divorced wife after she has remarried
N357: Not having relations with woman subject to Levirate marriage
N358: Not divorcing woman he has raped and been compelled to marry
N359: Not divorcing a woman after falsely bringing evil name on her
N360: Man incapable of procreation not to marry a Jewess
N361: Not to castrate a man or beast
N362: Not appointing a non- Israelite born King
N363: A king not owning many horses
N364: A king not taking many wives
N365: A king not amassing great personal wealth

Resurrection Vs Resuscitation: 20 Differences

Domenic Marbaniang

Published in *Christian Trends*, 2014

One important question in connection with the resurrection of Jesus asks how the resurrection of Jesus can be different from any other instance of a person coming back to life. For certain, there are numerable cases of people being resuscitated by medical means and cases of those who were raised from the dead supernaturally. The Bible also records cases of people who were raised from the dead: the son of the widow of Zarapeth, raised by Elijah in 1 Kings 17:7-24; Jairus's daughter in Matthew 9:18-26, the son of the widow of Nain in Luke 7:11-17, and Lazarus in John 11:38-44, raised by Jesus; Tabitha in Acts 9:40 by Peter, and Eutychus by Paul in Acts 20:7-12.

For the sake of this article, and for the benefit of theological distinction, let's call the other cases of people coming back to life, in the same body that they died, as "resuscitation" and distinguish it from the "resurrection" of Jesus Christ.
In this article we will point at 20 differences between resurrection and resuscitation (which term, only for the sake of this article, includes also miraculous reviving of the body, but not in the order of the resurrection of Jesus).

1. The resurrection of Jesus was permanent and everlasting (Rom.6:9); however, resuscitation was temporary. Even those who were raised from the dead in the Bible died a mortal's death later on.

2. The resurrection of Jesus transformed His flesh in a supernatural way. Jesus could pass through locked doors (John 20:19), travel faster than anything (Matt.28:7), and was free from the laws of nature (1Cor.15:44); however, in resuscitation there is no such change in the human body.

3. The resurrection of Jesus transformed His body to become imperishable, glorious, invincible, and spiritual (1Cor.15:42-44); in resuscitation, the body still is perishable, vile, and subject to the material laws of thermodynamics.

4. The resurrection of Jesus transformed His body for ascension to the right hand of God as the Second Man and as heir of all things (1Cor.15:47-50; Rom.1:4; Heb.1:2-4; Rev.19:15); the resuscitated body in its unchanged condition cannot inherit the kingdom of God (1Cor.15:50).

5. In His resurrection Jesus became the firstfruits of those who have fallen asleep [died] (1Cor.15:20,23); all those raised from the dead otherwise are not counted as part of this order of "new creation" resurrection.

6. In His resurrection, Jesus became the antitype of Adam; so that while in the latter all died because of his sin, now through the righteousness of Christ those who believe in Him will be made alive (1Cor.15:22; Rom.5:17,18). Resuscitation is the mere reviving of a body without any connection to the typology of Adam.

7. In His resurrection, Jesus became the author of new life (Rom.6:4); resuscitations are only revival to the old Adamic life, biologically speaking.

8. In His resurrection, Jesus conquered death so that death has no longer any dominion over Him (Rom.6:9; 8:3; 1Cor.15:55-57); all the others who were only resuscitated were still subject to physical death.

9. Jesus claimed that He had power to lay down His life and take it back again (John 10:18); those raised otherwise cannot make that claim.

10. The death and resurrection of Jesus had cosmic ("in Him"), creational ("die..,live"), and salvific ("those who believe") significance (Rom.7:4); the raising from the dead of others had no cosmic, creational, and salvific significance.

11. The death and resurrection of Jesus was eschatological, in that it was the firstfruits that guaranteed, at the end of the age, the resurrection of those who

    died in Christ (1Cor.15:23,24,26); that of those raised otherwise had no such eschatological significance.

12. The resurrection of Jesus was in the power and might of the Holy Spirit (Rom.1:4; 8:11; Phil.3:10) – remember, the angel didn't roll away the stone for Jesus to get out, but for the women to get in; in raising from the dead, otherwise, the body would still be weak (Mark 5:43; John 11:44).

13. Jesus' body was sown in weakness but raised in power (1Cor.15:43); in resuscitations, the body may not even be considered sown and raised in such categories that can only be applied to the resurrection of Jesus, the resuscitated body is still weak.

14. The resurrection of Jesus transformed His body to become free from the need of physical sustenance by food and drink (though, He could still eat, Luke 24:42,43); those raised otherwise still needed food, drink, shelter, and air to live (Mark 5:43).

15. The resurrection of Jesus provided hope of eternal life and defined the totality of the Gospel (1Cor.15:17-20); the resuscitations of others were just personal experiences.

16. In the resurrection of Jesus, His body was transformed according to the supernatural energetic power by which He subdues all things unto Himself (Phil.3:21); the resuscitations only revived the body but didn't subdue anything.

17. The resurrection of Jesus is the soteriological ground for the Holy Spirit to work in our bodies to give us victory over sin (Rom.8:11-14); the other resuscitations were mere physical reviving of bodies with no soteriological significance.

18. The resurrection of Jesus was a sign of life or death – it obligated people to a response in the Crucified and Risen Savior (Matt.12:39,40; Rom.10:9; 1Pet.1:21); the resuscitations were not necessary signs of any such or other kind
    – for instance, in the parable of the Rich Man and Lazarus, Abraham didn't respond to the rich man's request to send Lazarus back from the dead as a sign;

    because according to him, the Scriptures had more authority than the testimony of someone raised from the dead (Luke 16:30,31).

19. The resurrection of Jesus made His body spiritual (1Cor.15:44), so that though He has flesh and bones (Luke 24:39), He is called a life-giving Spirit (1Cor.15:45); but, those merely resuscitated are still raised in their natural (breathing, Gr. *psuchikos*) bodies subject to the laws of physical nature. (Note the contrast in 1Cor.15:45, "The first man Adam became a breathing creature, the last Adam became a life-giving spirit" (rendition mine), suggesting that the resurrected body of Jesus is not a breathing but a fully spiritual body).

20. The resurrection of Jesus is the ontological basis for not only the resurrection of those who die in Him, but also for the glorification of the bodies of those who are still alive at His coming (1Cor.15:51,52; Phil.3:21; 1Jn.3:2); the resuscitations were only shadowy and unparticular and anyone raised from the dead, not in order of the resurrection of Jesus, can only be saved and glorified by becoming part of the eschatological resurrection that the resurrection of Jesus provides ground for and promises, i.e., the resurrection of new creation (Heb.11:35).

THE FIVE COVENANTS OF SCRIPTURE

A Divine Biblical Covenant is a promise from God, formalised in a legal framework, solemnised by sacrifice and guaranteed by oath.

The five Covenants are stepping stones through time as God brings history to a climax in the Millennium in the restoration of all things that were lost through man's sin in Eden's garden.
(The word "unconditional" below refers to the certainty of the fulfilment of the divine promise in a covenant, but not necessarily the individual enjoyment of its blessing)

The COVENANTS	Refs	Type	Duration	Sign Symbol	Sacrifice	Timing	Beneficiary	Purpose
Noahic 2,348 BC	Genesis 6:18 8:20-22 9:8-18	Royal grant One-way Unilateral Unconditional	Everlasting	Rainbow (Gen 9:13-17)	Genesis 8:20-22	Inaugurated just after the cataclysmic worldwide destruction of the flood.	Made with Noah and his seed (with all of humanity and the animal kingdom).	To secure the earth as a **STAGE** for the restitution of all things (Acts 3:21) when all will be administered by Christ in Millennial Kingdom (Eph 1:10-11).
Abrahamic 1,913 BC	Genesis 12:1-3 15:13-18 17:9-11, 19 22:15-18	Royal grant One-way Unilateral Unconditional	Everlasting	Circumcision (Gen 17:11)	Genesis 15:8-21	Inaugurated just after the disaster of Nimrod's rebellion, the sin of "the sons of God" and the Tower of Babel.	Made with Abraham and His seed (Israel). Its spiritual blessings are enjoyed by believers now by faith.	To secure an innumerable **SEED** to enjoy the land and blessing (and the world through them). Not yet fulfilled but will come to pass in the Millennial Kingdom at Christ's second coming (Luke 1:71-75, Rom 4:13)
Mosaic - Old - Sinaitic 1,491 BC	Exodus 19:5-8 24:3-8 31:13-17	Suzerain Two-way Bilateral Conditional	Temporary (BC 1,500 to AD 32). Renewed 7x (eg. "Land Covenant" of Deut 29)	The Sabbath (Exod 31:13)	Exodus 24:4-8	Brought in just after the dramatic birth of Israel as they left Egypt. Abolished in the death of Christ (Heb 7:12-18, 8:13, 10:13)	Made with Israel. Written on stone. The Mosaic covenant has no connection with the church.	Added as a temporary supervisor to teach righteous **STANDARDS** and magnify sin until Christ came (Gal 3:22-26). No longer in force (2 Cor 3:9-11).
Davidic 1,042 BC	2 Samuel 7:11-16 Psalm 89:3-37	Royal grant One-way Unilateral Unconditional	Everlasting	Christ's resurrection and enthronement (Acts 2:30-33)	2 Samuel 6:17-18	Inaugurated between the past chaos of the "judges period" and the future apostasy of Israel and Judah in the post-Solomon era of a divided Kingdom of Israel.	Made with King David and his royal seed.	Secures a son of David as **SOVEREIGN**, to sit on a throne and reign for ever (Luke 1:32). Currently "dormant" but remains in place to be taken up when the Son of David (Christ) ascends David's throne in the Millennium.
Messianic - New - Second - Better - Everlasting 33 AD	Isa 59:20-21 Jer 31:31-34 Eze 36:24-31 37:26-38 Heb 8:8-12 10:15-18	Royal grant, One-way Unilateral Unconditional	Everlasting	Bread and cup (Matt 26:28, 1 Cor 11:25)	Hebrews 10:8-25, 29 12:24, 13:20	Announced in 606BC at the time of the Babylonian captivity. Then inaugurated on the darkest day in human history, the day when the Lord Jesus was crucified.	Enjoyed by believers spiritually now. To be nationally enjoyed by ethnic converted Israel at Christ's return, both spiritually and physically (Jer 31:31-34, Eze 36:24-31, 37:14-28, 39:25-29).	Replaces Old Covenant (Jer 31:31, Heb 7:18-19, 8:13). Secures **SALVATION**, a new heart and forgiveness for all of God's people (Heb 8:10-11). Includes a return to the land and peace for future converted Israel, ensuring they never again lose it through disobedience.

The above Covenant programme contains "Biblical covenants" only. It is not to be confused with what is popularly known as "Covenant Theology", which is a framework constructed by Reformed theologians in the 16th and 17th Centuries. "Covenant Theology" posits three "theological covenants", namely the "Covenant of Redemption" (made between the Father and the Son before creation), the "Covenant of Works" (made with Adam in the Garden of Eden) and the Covenant of Grace (promised in Gen 3:15 just after the fall), none of which are actually called 'covenants' in the Bible. Furthermore, Covenant Theology does not distinguish between Israel and the Church, nor does it see a literal 1,000 year future Kingdom on earth. For these reasons, Covenant Theology represents an inadequate framework for understanding the true Biblical "covenant programme".

Michael J Penfold 2021   webtruth.org

Made in the USA
Columbia, SC
23 June 2023